L23

Manual handling

Manual Handling Operations Regulations 1992
(as amended)

GUIDANCE ON REGULATIONS

D0544154

HSEBOOKS

© Crown copyright 2004

First published 1992
Second edition 1998
Third edition 2004

ISBN 0 7176 2823 X

This guidance is issued by the Health and Safety Executive. Following the guidance is not compulsory and you are free to take other action. But if you do follow the guidance you will normally be doing enough to comply with the law. Health and safety inspectors seek to secure compliance with the law and may refer to this guidance as illustrating good practice.

Contents

Introduction

1   This booklet aims to help employers, managers, safety officers, safety representatives, employees and others reduce the risk of injury from manual handling. It gives general guidance on the Manual Handling Operations Regulations 1992, as amended by the Health and Safety (Miscellaneous Amendments) Regulations 2002[1] ('the Regulations').

2   The Regulations originally came into force on 1 January 1993 and are made under the Health and Safety at Work etc Act 1974[2] (the HSW Act). They implement European Directive 90/269/EEC[3] on the manual handling of loads; supplement the general duties placed on employers and others by the HSW Act and the broad requirements of the Management of Health and Safety at Work Regulations 1999 (the Management Regulations);[4] and replace a number of earlier, outdated legal provisions.

3   There was only a small change to the Regulations in the 2002 amendment to better integrate a number of factors, from European Directive 90/269/EEC on the manual handling of loads, into the Regulations. These factors (in Annex II of the Directive) are that a worker may be if at risk if he/she:

(a)   is physically unsuited to carry out the task in question;

(b)   is wearing unsuitable clothing, footwear or other personal effects;

(c)   does not have adequate or appropriate knowledge or training.

4   These factors were in Schedule 1 of the 1992 Regulations (reproduced in this booklet) and are now included in a new regulation 4(3). This amendment does not introduce any new duties on employers.

5   The guidance has also been revised in other places, to bring it up to date with improvements in the knowledge of the risks from manual handling and how to avoid them. However, the main messages about the actions employers and workers should take to prevent risks have altered very little.

6   The Regulations apply to a wide range of manual handling activities involving the transporting or supporting of a load. This includes lifting, lowering, pushing, pulling, carrying or moving. The load may be either inanimate, for example, a box or a trolley, or animate, for example, a person or an animal. The risks from manual handling can be found across all workplaces, from offices to care homes and from factories to warehouses.

Scale of the problem

7   The most recent survey of self-reported work-related illness estimated that 1.1 million people in Britain suffered from musculoskeletal disorders (MSDs) in 2001/02, including those caused by manual handling. These account for around half of all work-related ill health. As a result of MSDs an estimated 12.3 million working days were lost in that year. In 1995/96, MSDs cost society £5.7 billion.

8   Manual handling accidents account for more than a third of all accidents reported each year to the enforcing authorities. While fatal manual handling accidents are rare, accidents resulting in a major injury are more common, accounting for 10.5% of the total number of reported manual handling accidents in 2001/02. The vast majority of reported manual handling accidents result in an over-three-day injury, most commonly a sprain or strain, often of the back. Figures 1 to 3 illustrate these patterns for over-three-day injuries reported in 2001/02. Manual handling injuries are part of a wider group of musculoskeletal problems; you may also find it helpful to refer to the Health and Safety Executive (HSE) booklet HSG60 *Upper limb disorders in the workplace*.[5]

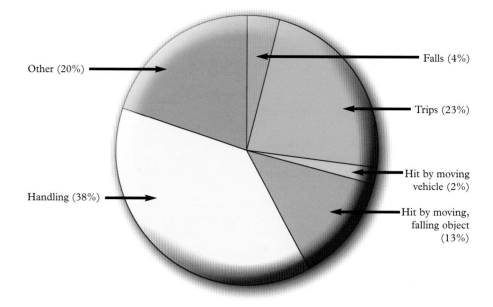

Other (20%)

Falls (4%)

Trips (23%)

Handling (38%)

Hit by moving
vehicle (2%)

Hit by moving,
falling object
(13%)

Figure 1 Kinds of accident causing over-three-day injury 2001/02

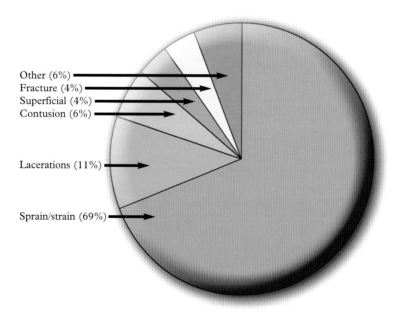

Other (6%)
Fracture (4%)
Superficial (4%)
Contusion (6%)

Lacerations (11%)

Sprain/strain (69%)

Figure 2 Types of over-three-day injury caused by manual handling accidents 2001/02

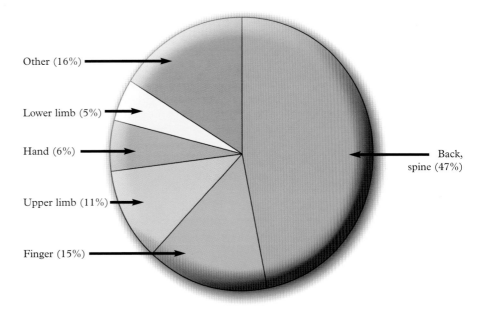

Other (16%)

Lower limb (5%)

Hand (6%)

Upper limb (11%)

Finger (15%)

Back,
spine (47%)

Figure 3 Sites of over-three-day injuries caused by handling accidents 2001/02

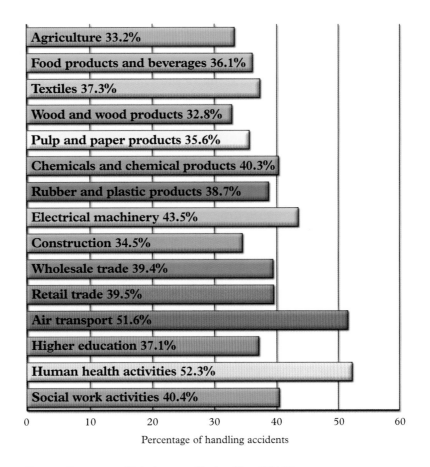

Agriculture 33.2%

Food products and beverages 36.1%

Textiles 37.3%

Wood and wood products 32.8%

Pulp and paper products 35.6%

Chemicals and chemical products 40.3%

Rubber and plastic products 38.7%

Electrical machinery 43.5%

Construction 34.5%

Wholesale trade 39.4%

Retail trade 39.5%

Air transport 51.6%

Higher education 37.1%

Human health activities 52.3%

Social work activities 40.4%

0   10   20   30   40   50   60

Percentage of handling accidents

Figure 4 Percentage of injuries caused by handling 2001/02

3

9   Figure 4, also based on over-three-day injuries reported in 2001/02, shows that the problem of manual handling is not confined to a narrow range of industries. Nor is the problem confined to 'industrial' work: for example, manual handling accounts for more than 39% of accidents in wholesale and retail distribution and 52% in the health services.

10 Because of the scale of the problem, prevention and control of MSDs is one of the priority programmes in the Health and Safety Commission's (HSC's) strategic plan. As so many people are at risk from manual handling injuries there is considerable potential for reducing the total amount of ill health if stakeholders such as employers, employees' safety representatives and trade unions take steps to:

(a)   comply with the Regulations and guidance;

(b)   review risk assessments as and when necessary;

(c)   encourage early reporting of symptoms;

(d)   ensure cases of manual handling injury are managed effectively; and

(e)   consult and involve the workforce. They know the risks and can offer solutions to control them.

11 The key messages from the HSC MSD priority programme are that:

(a)   there are things that can be done to prevent or minimise MSDs;

(b)   the prevention measures are cost effective;

(c)   you cannot prevent all MSDs, so early reporting of symptoms, proper treatment and suitable rehabilitation is essential.

12 There is evidence that heavy manual labour, awkward postures, manual handling, and a previous or existing injury are all risk factors in the development of MSDs. The injured person may not always make a full recovery; this may depend on the treatment and advice that they receive. Information on how to manage back pain in the workplace is available from HSE's website and in *The back book*.[6]

13 There is now substantial acceptance of both the scale of manual handling problems and methods of prevention. Modern medical and scientific knowledge stresses the importance of an ergonomic approach to remove or reduce the risk of manual handling injury. Ergonomics is sometimes described as 'fitting the job to the person, rather than the person to the job'. The ergonomic approach looks at manual handling as a whole. It takes into account a range of relevant factors, including the nature of the task, the load, the working environment and individual capability and requires worker participation. This approach is central to the European Directive on manual handling, and to the Regulations.

14 As mentioned, physical risk factors can be harmful to the body and can lead to people developing MSDs. However, research has shown that psychosocial risk factors also need to be taken into account. These are things that may affect workers' psychological response to their work and workplace conditions (including working relationships with supervisors and colleagues). Examples are high workloads, tight deadlines, and lack of control of the work and working methods.

Legal context

15   The Regulations should not be considered in isolation. Regulation 3(1) of the Management Regulations requires employers to make a suitable and sufficient assessment of the risks to the health and safety of their employees while at work. Where this general assessment indicates the possibility of risks to employees from the manual handling of loads, the requirements of the present Regulations should be followed.

16   The Regulations establish a clear hierarchy of measures:

(a)   Avoid hazardous manual handling operations so far as is reasonably practicable. This may be done by redesigning the task to avoid moving the load or by automating or mechanising the process.

(b)   Make a suitable and sufficient assessment of any hazardous manual handling operations that cannot be avoided.

(c)   Reduce the risk of injury from those operations so far as is reasonably practicable. Where possible, mechanical assistance should be provided, for example, a sack trolley or hoist. Where this is not reasonably practicable then changes to the task, the load and the working environment should be explored.

17   **The Regulations set no specific requirements such as weight limits.** The ergonomic approach shows clearly that such requirements are based on too simple a view of the problem and may lead to incorrect conclusions. Instead, an ergonomic assessment based on a range of relevant factors is used to determine the risk of injury and point the way to remedial action.

18   The law also requires employers to consult their employees on matters that affect their health and safety. Where an employer recognises a trade union, then the Safety Representatives and Safety Committees Regulations (SRSCR) 1977,[7] provide for the appointment of trade union safety representatives. Under the SRSCR, the employer is required to consult these safety representatives on matters that affect the health and safety of the employees they represent. The SRSCR also specify the functions of such safety representatives and set out the obligations of employers towards them. All other onshore employers have a duty to consult their employees under the Health and Safety (Consultation with Employees) Regulations (HSCER) 1996.[8] Under the HSCER, the employer can choose how they consult their employees, either directly with each employee or through elected representatives of employee safety. The HSCER specify the functions of such representatives and set out the obligations of employers towards them.

19   Where it is not possible to avoid a manual handling operation then employers have to assess any risks to the health of their employees. However, a full assessment of every manual handling operation could be a major undertaking and might involve wasted effort. To enable assessment work to be concentrated where it is most needed, Appendix 3 gives numerical guidelines which can be used as an initial filter. This will help to identify those manual handling operations which need a more detailed examination. However, even manual handling operations which are within the guidelines should be avoided or made less demanding wherever it is reasonably practicable to do so. **Do not regard the guidelines as precise recommendations. Where there is doubt make a more detailed assessment.**

20   This booklet contains general guidance within which individual industries and sectors will be able to produce more specific guidance appropriate to their own circumstances.

Regulation 1

**Regulation
1**

Citation and commencement

These Regulations may be cited as the Manual Handling Operations Regulations 1992 and shall come into force on 1 January 1993.

Regulation 2

Regulation

2(1)

Interpretation

(1)   In these Regulations, unless the context otherwise requires –

"injury" does not include injury caused by any toxic or corrosive substance which –

> *(a)   has leaked or spilled from a load;*

> *(b)   is present on the surface of a load but has not leaked or spilled from it; or*

> *(c)   is a constituent part of a load;*

and "injured" shall be construed accordingly;

"load" includes any person and any animal;

"manual handling operations" means any transporting or supporting of a load (including the lifting, putting down, pushing, pulling, carrying or moving thereof) by hand or by bodily force.

Guidance

2(1)

Definitions of certain terms

Injury

21   The main aim of the Regulations is to prevent injury, not only to the back, but to any part of the body. They require employers to take into account the whole handling operation including the external physical properties of loads which might either affect grip or cause direct injury, for example, slipperiness, roughness, sharp edges and extremes of temperature.

22   Hazards which result from any toxic or corrosive properties of the load are not covered by the Regulations. Hazards which result from spillage or leakage are likely to be subject to the Control of Substances Hazardous to Health Regulations 2002[9] (COSHH). For example, the presence of oil on the surface of a load is relevant to the Regulations if it makes the load slippery to handle, but the risk of dermatitis from contact with the oil is dealt with by COSHH.

Load

23   A load in this context must be a discrete movable object. This includes, for example, not only packages and boxes but also a patient receiving medical attention, an animal during husbandry or undergoing veterinary treatment, and material supported on a shovel or fork. An implement, tool or machine, such as a chainsaw, fire hose or breathing apparatus, is not considered to be a load when in use for its intended purpose.

Manual handling operations

24   The Regulations apply to the manual handling of loads, ie by human effort, as opposed to mechanical handling by crane, lift trucks etc. The human

effort may be applied directly to the load, or indirectly by hauling on a rope or pulling on a lever. Introducing mechanical assistance, for example a sack truck or a powered hoist, may reduce but not eliminate manual handling since human effort is still required to move, steady or position the load.

25 Manual handling includes both transporting a load and supporting a load in a static posture. The load may be moved or supported by the hands or any other part of the body, for example, the shoulder. Manual handling also includes the intentional dropping of a load and the throwing of a load, whether into a container or from one person to another.

26 The application of human effort for a purpose other than transporting or supporting a load is not a manual handling operation. For example, turning the starting handle of an engine or lifting a control lever on a machine is not manual handling, nor is the action of pulling on a rope while lashing down cargo on the back of a vehicle.

Regulation
2(2)

(2) Any duty imposed by these Regulations on an employer in respect of his employees shall also be imposed on a self-employed person in respect of himself.

Duties of the self-employed

27 Regulation 2(2) makes the self-employed responsible for their own safety during manual handling. They should take the same steps to safeguard themselves as employers must to protect their employees, in similar circumstances. Employers should remember, however, that they may be responsible for the health and safety of someone who is self-employed for tax and National Insurance purposes but who works under their control and direction (see paragraphs 38-40).

Regulation 3

Disapplication of Regulations

These Regulations shall not apply to or in relation to the master or crew of a sea-going ship or to the employer of such persons in respect of the normal ship-board activities of a ship's crew under the direction of the master.

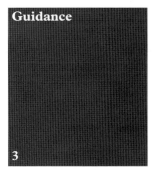

Sea-going ships

28 Sea-going ships are subject to separate Merchant Shipping legislation administered by the Maritime and Coastguard Agency. The Regulations, therefore, do not apply to the normal ship-board activities of a ship's crew under the direction of the master. However, the Regulations may apply to other manual handling operations aboard a ship, for example, where a shore-based contractor carries out the work, provided the ship is within territorial waters. The Regulations also apply to certain activities carried out offshore (see regulation 7).

Regulation 4

Duties of employers

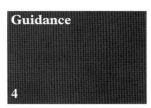

Introduction

29 The Regulations should not be considered in isolation. Regulation 3(1) of the Management Regulations requires employers to make a suitable and sufficient assessment of the risks to the health and safety of their employees while at work. Where this general assessment indicates the possibility of risks

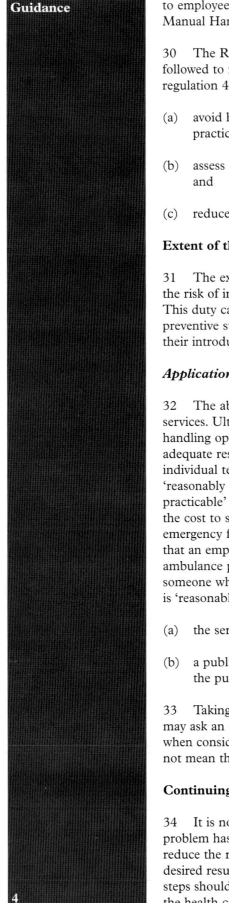

to employees from the manual handling of loads, the requirements of the Manual Handling Operations Regulations should be complied with.

30 The Regulations set out a hierarchy of measures which should be followed to reduce the risks from manual handling. These are set out in regulation 4(1) and are as follows:

(a) avoid hazardous manual handling operations so far as is reasonably practicable;

(b) assess any hazardous manual handling operations that cannot be avoided; and

(c) reduce the risk of injury so far as is reasonably practicable.

Extent of the employer's duties

31 The extent of the employer's duty to avoid manual handling or to reduce the risk of injury is determined by reference to what is 'reasonably practicable'. This duty can be satisfied if the employer can show that the cost of any further preventive steps would be grossly disproportionate to the further benefit from their introduction.

Application to the emergency services

32 The above approach is fully applicable to the work of the emergency services. Ultimately, the cost of prohibiting all potentially hazardous manual handling operations would be an inability to provide the general public with an adequate rescue service. However, the interests of society and the endangered individual tend to conflict with the interests of the manual handler and what is 'reasonably practicable' may not be easy to ascertain. What is 'reasonably practicable' for a fire authority, for example, would need to take into account the cost to society where any further preventive steps would make its emergency functions extremely difficult to perform. Recent case law suggests that an employee whose job may involve lifting people (for example, ambulance personnel) may be asked to accept a greater risk of injury than someone who is employed to move inanimate objects. When considering what is 'reasonably practicable', additional potentially relevant factors may be:

(a) the seriousness of the need for the lifting operation; and

(b) a public authority's duties to the public and to the particular member of the public who has called for the authority's help.

33 Taking these factors into account, the level of risk which an employer may ask an employee to accept may, in appropriate circumstances, be higher when considering the health and safety of those in danger, although this does not mean that employees can be exposed to unacceptable risk of injury.

Continuing nature of the duty

34 It is not sufficient simply to make changes and then hope that the problem has been dealt with. The steps taken to avoid manual handling or reduce the risk of injury should be monitored to check that they are having the desired result. If they are not then alternatives will need to be found. Such steps should be in line with current best practice and technology (especially in the health care sector) as practices change.

35   Regulation 4(2) (see paragraph 176) requires the assessment made under regulation 4(1) to be kept up to date.

Work away from the employer's premises

36   The Regulations impose duties on employers whose employees carry out manual handling. However, manual handling operations may occur away from the employer's premises, for example, delivering goods, or providing personal care, in situations where the employer has more limited control. Where possible the employer should liaise closely with those in control of the premises where the deliveries are made or care is given to enable them to plan how the work can be done safely. There will sometimes be a limit to employers' ability to influence the working environment, but the task and perhaps the load will often remain within their control, as will the provision of effective training, so it is still possible to establish a safe system of work for manual handling which takes place away from the employer's own premises.

37   Employers and others in charge of premises where visiting employees work also have duties towards those employees, particularly under sections 3 or 4 of the HSW Act, the Management Regulations and the Workplace (Health, Safety and Welfare) Regulations 1992[10] (as amended). For example, they need to ensure that the premises and plant provided there are in a safe condition.

Those self-employed for tax/National Insurance purposes

38   Individuals working under the control and direction of another may be regarded as employees for health and safety purposes even though they are treated as self-employed for tax/National Insurance purposes. Those who employ workers on this basis, therefore, may need to take appropriate action to protect them. If any doubt exists about who is responsible for the health and safety of such workers, legal advice should be sought.

39   Although only the courts can give an authoritative interpretation of the law, in considering the application of the Regulations and guidance to people working under another's direction, whether or not the worker is an employee will depend on the details of the relationship between the parties involved. The following factors are among those likely to be relevant:

(a)   the degree of control exercised over the worker;

(b)   whether the worker can properly be regarded as part of the employer's organisation;

(c)   whether the 'employer' has the power to select and appoint the individuals doing the work;

(d)   whether the 'employer' has the power to dismiss or suspend the worker;

(e)   the way wages or salary are paid and whether holiday pay is paid;

(f)   who supplies the worker's equipment;

(g)   who fixes the time and place of work;

(h)   whether the worker is able to delegate performance of his or her duties;

(i)   whether the 'employer' deducts income tax and National Insurance; and

(j)   the intention of the parties involved.

40   Recent case law held that whether a worker was also an employee can only be determined from a full consideration of all the evidence, including all the relevant evidence about the dynamics of the working relationship between the parties, regardless of the label given to that relationship by the parties.

(1)   Each employer shall –

(a)   so far as is reasonably practicable, avoid the need for his employees to undertake any manual handling operations at work which involve a risk of their being injured.

Avoiding manual handling

41   If the general assessment carried out under regulation 3(1) of the Management Regulations indicates a possibility of injury from manual handling operations, the first thing to consider is whether the manual handling operation can be avoided altogether. It may not be necessary to assess the risk in great detail, particularly if the operations can easily be avoided or the appropriate steps to reduce any risk of injury to the lowest level reasonably practicable are obvious. Appendix 3 provides some simple numerical guidelines to assist with this initial judgement, at least in relatively straightforward cases.

Elimination of handling

42   When trying to avoid manual handling the first questions to ask are whether the load/s need to be handled at all, or could the work be done in a different way? For example, can a process such as machining or wrapping be carried out *in situ*, without handling the loads? Can a treatment be brought to a patient rather than taking the patient to the treatment?

Automation or mechanisation

43   If, so far as is reasonably practicable, handling of the load cannot be avoided, then can the operation/s be either:

(a)   automated; or

(b)   mechanised?

44   Remember that the introduction of automation or mechanisation may create other, different risks. Even automated plant will require maintenance and repair. Mechanisation, for example by the introduction of lift trucks or powered conveyors, may introduce different risks requiring precautions of their own.

45   Decisions on the use of mechanisation or automation are best made when plant or systems of work are being designed. Raw materials can be handled in the workplace in ways that eliminate or reduce the need for manual handling. For example, powders or liquids can be transferred from large containers and big bags by gravity feed or pneumatic transfer, avoiding bag or container handling. The layout of the process can often be designed to minimise transfer of materials or the distance over which containers have to be moved. Examination of existing activities may also reveal opportunities for avoiding manual handling operations that involve a risk of injury. Such improvements often bring additional benefits in terms of greater efficiency and productivity, and reduced damage to loads.

(1) Each employer shall –

(b) where it is not reasonably practicable to avoid the need for his employees to undertake any manual handling operations at work which involve a risk of their being injured –

(i) make a suitable and sufficient assessment of all such manual handling operations to be undertaken by them, having regard to the factors which are specified in column 1 of Schedule 1 to these Regulations and considering the questions which are specified in the corresponding entry in column 2 of that Schedule,

(ii) take appropriate steps to reduce the risk of injury to those employees arising out of their undertaking any such manual handling operations to the lowest level reasonably practicable, and

(iii) take appropriate steps to provide any of those employees who are undertaking any such manual handling operations with general indications and, where it is reasonably practicable to do so, precise information on –

(aa) the weight of each load, and

(bb) the heaviest side of any load whose centre of gravity is not positioned centrally.

4(1)(b)

Guidance

Assessment of risk, risk reduction and information on the load

46 The guidance on regulation 4(1)(b) is in four parts:

(a) General advice on manual handling risk assessment – regulation 4(1)(b)(i) (paragraphs 47-71).

(b) General principles for reducing manual handling risks – regulation 4(1)(b)(ii) (paragraphs 72-84).

(c) Practical advice on assessing and reducing risks in manual handling, discussed under various aspects of the task, the load and the working environment – regulation 4(1)(b)(i) and (ii) (paragraphs 85-171).

(d) Guidance on providing additional information on the load – regulation 4(1)(b)(iii) (paragraphs 172-175).

4(1)(b)

General advice on manual handling risk assessment

Guidance

Use of generic manual handling assessments

47 Employers' assessments will be 'suitable and sufficient' as long as they have considered:

(a) all the types of manual handling operations their employees are required to carry out; and

(b) any relevant individual factors covered by regulation 4(3).

4(1)(b)(i)

48 'Generic' assessments based on risks which are common to a number of broadly similar operations are quite acceptable, however, they should consider all of the manual handling risks that are present in these operations. If the assessment is based on a narrow selection of operations, some manual handling risks may be missed. The findings should be made available to all the employees to whom it applies and to the relevant safety representatives.

49 An assessment made at the last minute is unlikely to be 'suitable and sufficient'. In carrying out assessments, employers, in consultation with their employees, need to use their experiences of the type of work being done. This approach will help particularly with the assessment of work which:

(a) is very varied (such as construction or maintenance); or

(b) is peripatetic (ie takes place at more than one location, for example, making deliveries); or

(c) involves dealing with emergencies (such as fire-fighting, rescue and medical emergencies).

50 In the case of delivery operations, for example, a useful technique is to list the various types of task, load and working environment concerned and then to review a selection of them. This can be done by starting at the beginning of the operation and working through step by step to the end point. The aim is to identify the range of manual handling risks to which employees are exposed and then to decide on any necessary preventive steps such as the use of handling aids.

51 A distinction should be made between the employer's assessment required by regulation 4(1)(b)(i) and the everyday judgements which supervisors and others will have to make in dealing with manual handling operations. The assessment should identify in broad terms the foreseeable problems likely to arise during the operations and the measures needed to deal with them. These measures should include the provision of training to enable supervisors and employees to cope effectively with the operations they are likely to undertake.

52 This distinction is perhaps most clearly seen in the case of emergency work. Here it will be essential to provide training to enable staff to carry out risk assessments which allow them to make the rapid judgements that will inevitably be necessary in dealing satisfactorily with an emergency incident or in supervising realistic training (dynamic risk assessment). The assessment may change rapidly as the emergency progresses. Clear communication between parties is vital in such situations.

53 In other areas, for example moving and handling people, a multi-staged risk assessment system may be applicable. A generic or task-based assessment should be undertaken to ensure that a unit, for example, is properly designed and equipped. Staff should be properly trained to meet the mobility needs of the expected patient/client group as safely as possible for all parties. In addition, an individual patient assessment will be required for those patients with significant mobility needs. Such an assessment is likely to change as the condition of the person alters and in line with decisions about therapies they may be undergoing, for example positioning for radiological examination. The assessment should identify what tasks will be necessary, who should carry them out and how that patient will be moved and handled. Ideally, the assessment should include specific information about ways the person may be able to assist with the manoeuvre themselves and also any handling equipment, for example hoists, slings or small aids to be used.

12

54   Risk assessment for moving/handling people is a complex task requiring consideration of the medical condition of the patient and the human rights of those involved. This guidance is not intended to provide comprehensive advice on these other issues. Further information is contained in HSG225 *Handling home care*.[11] Ideally this assessment should be carried out before admission to ensure suitable equipment is available on the admitting unit. Staff must be trained to recognise what they can and cannot handle safely in each unit. Information must be available to the staff carrying out the assessment about what equipment is available and how to access it.

Employees' contribution

55   Employers have a duty to consult safety representatives, elected representatives of employees' safety and employees about the arrangements they make for health and safety in the workplace. This includes any risk-prevention strategy. But for this to be successful, it is essential that employers work in partnership with safety representatives and employees, because they know at first hand the risks in the workplace and can offer practical solutions to controlling them. Safety representatives can make a particular contribution because of the specialised training and support they receive, which helps them to understand workplace risks and to develop ways to control them. For example, safety representatives and employees can make effective contributions by bringing to the employer's attention the difficulties caused by:

(a)   the size or shape of loads;

(b)   how often loads are handled;

(c)   the order in which the task is carried out;

(d)   the environment in which the handling operations are carried out, for example:

(i)   any space constraints which make it difficult to manoeuvre the load;

(ii)   unsuitable shelving/storage systems;

(iii)   uneven flooring.

Need for an assessment

56   Where the general assessment carried out under regulation 3(1) of the Management Regulations indicates a possibility of injury from manual handling operations, but the conclusion reached under regulation 4(1)(a) of the Manual Handling Operations Regulations is that avoidance of the operations is not reasonably practicable, a more specific assessment should be carried out as required by regulation 4(1)(b)(i).

How detailed should this assessment be?

57   How detailed this further assessment needs to be will depend on the circumstances. Appendix 3 includes some simple numerical guidelines which are intended to be used as an initial filter, to help identify those operations which need a more detailed assessment.

58   Regulation 4(3) and Schedule 1 to the Regulations set out the factors which the assessment should take into account, including the **task**, the **load**,

13

the **working environment** and **individual capability**. First, a decision needs to be made on how the assessment is to be done, who is going to do it and what relevant information may already be available to help.

Who should carry out the assessment?

59   Assessment may best be carried out by members of staff who are familiar with the operations in question, as long as they have the competencies to do so. It may be necessary to call in outside expertise where, for example, the manual handling operation being carried out is complex. Before in-house personnel are allowed to act as assessors, suitable checks should be made during and after training to ensure that the individuals have understood the information given to them and have reached an adequate level of competence. (One way to do this would be for the trainer to observe the assessor at work and to review a sample of written assessments.)

60   Those responsible for assessment should be familiar with the main requirements of the Regulations and have the ability to:

(a)   identify hazards (including less obvious ones) and assess risks from the type of manual handling being done;

(b)   use additional sources of information on risks as appropriate;

(c)   draw valid and reliable conclusions from assessments and identify steps to reduce risks;

(d)   make a clear record of the assessment and communicate the findings to those who need to take appropriate action, and to the worker(s) concerned;

(e)   recognise their own limitations as to assessment so that further expertise can be called on if necessary.

61   While one individual may be able to carry out a perfectly satisfactory assessment, at least in relatively straightforward cases, it can be helpful to draw on the knowledge and expertise of others. In some organisations this is done informally, while others prefer to set up a small assessment team. Areas of knowledge and expertise likely to be relevant to successful risk assessment of manual handling operations, and individuals who may be able to make a useful contribution are shown in Table 1.

62   It may be appropriate to seek outside help, for example, to give training to in-house assessors or where manual handling risks are novel or particularly difficult to assess. Possible sources of such help are given in the 'Useful contacts' section. Outside specialist advice may also help solve unusual handling problems or contribute to ergonomic design. But employers should oversee the assessment as they have the final responsibility for it.

Records of accidents and ill health

63   Well-kept records of accidents and ill health can play a useful part in the assessment process. They should identify and document any accidents associated with manual handling. Careful analysis may also show evidence of any links between manual handling and ill health, including injuries apparently unrelated to any specific event or accident. Other possible indicators of manual handling problems include:

(a) high levels of absenteeism or staff turnover;

(b) poor productivity and morale;

(c) excessive product damage;

(d) unwillingness by employees to perform a specific task or tasks; and

(e) general dissatisfaction among the employees concerned.

64   However, such indicators are not a complete guide and should be used only to supplement other risk assessment methods.

Table 1 Who to involve in the risk assessment

Knowledge and expertise required	People who may be able to help
Requirements of the Regulations	Manager, health and safety professional, ergonomist, safety representatives
Nature of the handling operations	Supervisor, industrial engineer, employees and safety representatives
A basic understanding of human capabilities	Occupational physician, occupational health nurse, health and safety professional, ergonomist, physiotherapist, occupational therapist, back care advisor
Identification of high-risk activities	Manager, supervisor, occupational health nurse, health and safety professional, ergonomist, physiotherapist, occupational therapist, back care advisor, employees and safety representatives
Practical steps to reduce risk	Manager, supervisor, industrial engineer, health and safety professional, ergonomist, physiotherapist, occupational therapist, back care advisor, suppliers, employees and safety representatives

Industry-specific data and assessments

65   Individual industries and sectors have a valuable role to play in identifying common manual handling problems and developing practical solutions. Trade associations and similar bodies can also act as a focus for the collection and analysis of accident and ill-health data drawn from a far wider base than that available to the individual employer.

Recording the assessment

66   In general, the significant findings of the assessment should be recorded and the record kept, readily accessible, as long as it remains relevant. However, the assessment need not be recorded if:

(a) it could very easily be repeated and explained at any time because it is simple and obvious; or

(b)   the manual handling operations are of low risk, are going to last only a very short time, and the time taken to record the assessment would be disproportionate.

Making a more detailed assessment

67   When a more detailed assessment is necessary it should follow the broad structure set out in Schedule 1 to the Regulations. The Schedule lists a number of questions in five categories including:

(a)   the **task**;

(b)   the **load**;

(c)   the **working environment**;

(d)   **individual capability** (this category is discussed in more detail under regulation 4(3) and its guidance); and

(e)   **other factors**, for example, use of protective clothing.

68   Not all of these questions will be relevant in every case. They are covered in the checklists (see paragraph 70 and Appendix 4). More detailed practical advice on points to consider for the first three categories is given in paragraphs 86-171.

69   Each of these categories may influence the others and none of them can be considered on their own. However, to carry out an assessment in a structured way it is often helpful to begin by breaking the operations down into separate, more manageable items.

Assessment checklist

70   It may be helpful to use a checklist during the assessment (see Appendix 4 for examples). These checklists cover both the analysis of risk required by regulation 4(1)(b)(i) and the identification of the steps to reduce the risk as required by regulation 4(1)(b)(ii), which is discussed later. The particular examples given will not be suitable in all circumstances and they can be adapted or modified as appropriate.

71   **Remember** – assessment is not an end in itself, only a structured way of analysing risks. It should enable the assessor, in consultation with the workforce, to develop practical solutions.

General principles for reducing manual handling risks

Striking a balance

72   In considering how best to reduce any risks found, the same structured approach which was used during the assessment of risk should be used. Consider in turn the **task**, the **load**, the **working environment** and **individual capability** (see regulation 4(3) and its guidance) as well as **other factors**.

73   The emphasis given to each of these factors may depend in part on the nature and circumstances of the manual handling operations. Routine manual handling operations carried out in essentially unchanging circumstances, for example in manufacturing processes, may lend themselves particularly to improvement of the task and working environment.

74   However, manual handling operations carried out in circumstances which change continually, for example certain activities carried out in mines or on construction sites, may offer less scope for improvement of the working environment and perhaps the task. More attention may, therefore, be given to the load, for example can it be made lighter or easier to handle?

75   For varied work of this kind, including much of the work of the emergency services and the healthcare sector, the provision of effective training will be especially important. It should enable employees to recognise potentially hazardous handling operations. It should also give them a clear understanding of why they should avoid or modify such operations where possible, make full use of appropriate equipment and apply good handling technique.

An ergonomic approach

76   Health, safety and productivity are most likely to be optimised if an ergonomic approach is used to design the manual handling operations as a whole. Wherever possible full consideration should be given to the **task**, the **load**, the **working environment**, **individual capability** (see regulation 4(3) and its guidance), **other factors** and the relationship between them, with a view to fitting the operations to the individual rather than the other way around.

77   While better job or workplace design may not eliminate handling injuries, the evidence is that it can greatly reduce them. **Consider providing mechanical assistance where this is reasonably practicable.**

Mechanical assistance

78   Mechanical assistance involves the use of handling aids – some manual handling is retained but bodily forces are applied more efficiently, reducing the risk of injury. There are many examples:

(a)   a simple lever can reduce the risk of injury by decreasing the bodily force required to move a load, or by removing fingers from a potentially damaging trap;

(b)   a hoist, either powered or hand-operated, can support the weight of a load and leave the handler free to control its position;

(c)   a trolley, sack truck or roller conveyor can greatly reduce the effort required to move a load horizontally;

(d)   chutes are a convenient way of using gravity to move loads from one place to another;

(e)   handling devices such as hand-held hooks or suction pads can simplify the problem of handling a load that is difficult to grasp.

79   Examples of some common handling aids are illustrated in Figures 5-14.

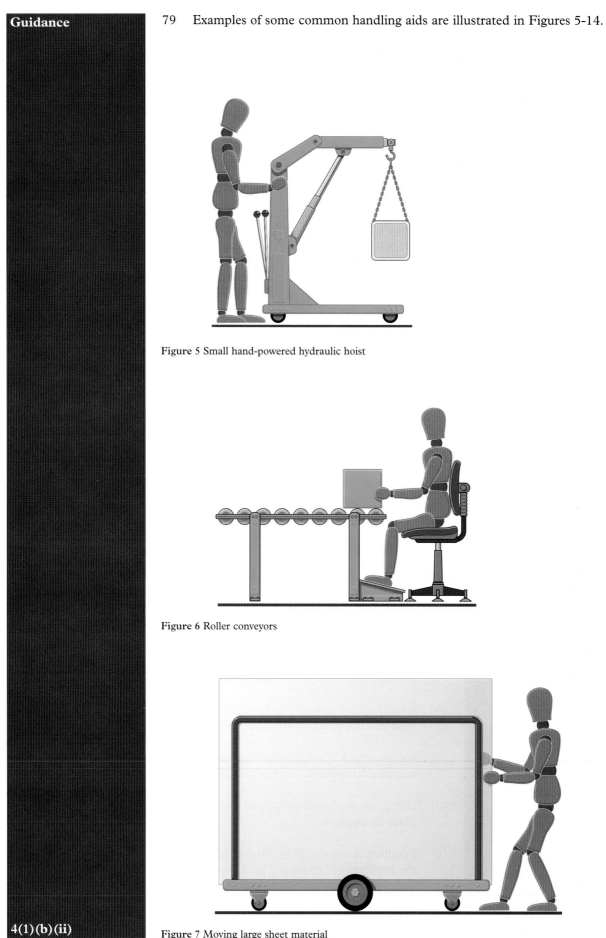

Figure 5 Small hand-powered hydraulic hoist

Figure 6 Roller conveyors

Figure 7 Moving large sheet material

Figure 8 Small hydraulic lorry loading crane

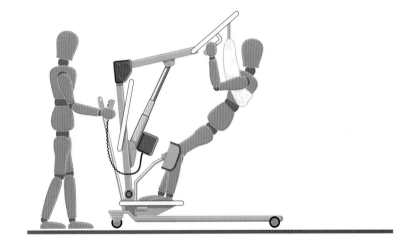

Figure 9 Patient standing hoist

Figure 10 The simple, low-tech sack trolley

Figure 11 Powered vacuum lifter

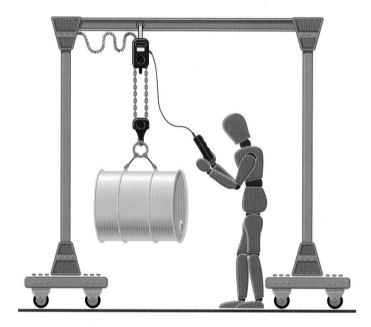

Figure 12 Electric hoist on mobile gantry

Figure 13 Truck with hydraulic lifting mechanism

Figure 14 Mobile welding set

80   All equipment provided for use during manual handling, including handling aids and personal protective equipment (PPE), should be included in a planned preventive maintenance programme which should include a defect reporting and correction system. Equipment should be readily accessible for the tasks it is to be used for. Handling aids and PPE that are not readily accessible are less likely to be used (see the Provision and Use of Work Equipment Regulations 1998,[12] the Lifting Operations and Lifting Equipment Regulations 1998[13] and Food Information Sheet FIS33 *Roll cages and wheeled racks in the food and drink industries: Reducing manual handling injuries*[14]).

Involving the workforce

81   Employees, their safety representatives and safety committees should be involved in any redesign of the system of work and encouraged to report any defects. They should also be involved in the development of good handling practice.

Industry-specific guidance

82   The development of industry-specific guidance within the framework established by the Regulations and this general guidance will provide a valuable source of information on preventive action that has been found effective for particular activities or types of work. This guidance is increasingly becoming available on HSE's website www.hse.gov.uk. Some examples of such guidance are given in the 'References' and 'Further reading' sections.

'Appropriate' steps

83   Above all, the steps taken to reduce the risk of injury should be 'appropriate'. They should address the problem in a practical and effective manner and their effectiveness should be monitored. This can be done by observing the effect of the changes made, and discussing these changes with the handlers or, less directly, by checking accident statistics regularly. If they do not have the desired effect the situation should be reappraised (see also paragraph 176).

Checklist

84   As in risk assessment, it may be helpful to use a checklist when looking for practical steps to reduce the risk of injury. The example of a checklist discussed earlier (see paragraph 70 and Appendix 4) combines the assessment of risk required by regulation 4(1)(b)(i) with the identification of remedial steps required by regulation 4(1)(b)(ii). The example given may not be suitable in all circumstances but it can be adapted or modified as appropriate.

Practical advice on assessing and reducing risks in manual handling

85   The following section contains additional practical advice on what to look for when making risk assessments of manual handling activities. It breaks these down according to various task factors, aspects of the load, and the working environment. Where appropriate, practical ways of taking action to reduce risks are discussed within each topic.

The task

Task layout

Is the load held or manipulated at a distance from the trunk?

86   As the load is moved away from the trunk the general level of stress on the lower back rises. Regardless of the handling technique used, not keeping the load close to the body will increase the stress. As a rough guide, holding a load at arm's length imposes about five times the stress experienced when holding the same load very close to the trunk. Figure 15 shows how individual handling capacity reduces as the hands move away from the trunk.

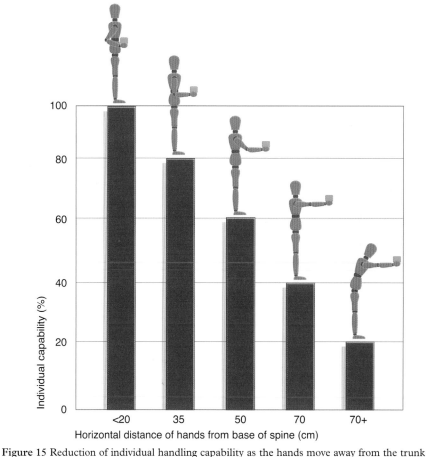

Figure 15 Reduction of individual handling capability as the hands move away from the trunk

22

87   Also, the further away the load, the less easy it is to control. Friction between the load and the worker's garments can help to support or steady the load. If the load is moved away from the body, this benefit is reduced or lost, and it is more difficult to counterbalance the load with the weight of the trunk.

Does the task involve twisting the trunk?

88   Stress on the lower back increases significantly if the trunk is twisted during manual handling. This stress is made worse if twisting occurs while lifting a load.

Does the task involve stooping?

89   Stooping can also increase the stress on the lower back. This happens whether the handler stoops by bending the back or by leaning forward with the back straight – in each case the trunk is thrown forward and its weight is added to the load being handled. However, stooping slightly may be preferable to adopting a squatting posture, which can place excessive loads on knees and hips.

Does the task involve reaching upwards?

90   Reaching upwards places additional stresses on the arms and back. Control of the load becomes more difficult and, because the arms are extended, they are more likely to be injured.

Does the task involve considerable lifting or lowering distances?

91   The distance through which a load is lifted or lowered can also be important: large distances are considerably more demanding physically than small ones. Also, lifting or lowering over a large distance is likely to need a change of grip during the operation, further increasing the risk of injury. Lifts beginning at floor level or above head height should be avoided where possible.

Does the task involve considerable carrying distances?

92   In general, if a load can safely be lifted and lowered, it can also be carried without endangering the back. However, if a load is carried for an excessive distance, physical stresses are prolonged, leading to fatigue and increased risk of injury. As a rough guide, if a load is carried further than about 10 m then the physical demands of carrying the load will tend to predominate over those of lifting and lowering and individual capability will be reduced.

Does the task involve considerable pushing or pulling of the load?

93   Most pushing and pulling workplace activities are introduced as a way of reducing manual handling, for example eliminating carrying by loading goods onto a trolley. However, lifting, lowering and carrying, pushing or pulling a load can harm the handler. The majority of injuries resulting from pushing and pulling activities affect the back, neck and shoulders. Entrapment injuries are also common. Approximately two-thirds of push/pull accidents involve objects that are not supported on wheels, for example, furniture or bales of wool.

94 Points to consider when reducing the risks from pushing and pulling include:

(a) the length of the route. Is this as short as possible?

(b) the number of journeys. Would it be safer to make repeated journeys rather than a few demanding ones?

(c) how demanding the work is;

(d) whether the route is clear of obstacles, including doorways;

(e) whether the floor surface is well maintained;

(f) whether the task involves negotiating kerbs, steps or slopes. Full use should be made of ramps etc.

95 The initial forces used to overcome the object's inertia when starting or changing direction are usually higher than the sustained forces used to keep the object moving and should therefore be kept to a minimum. Frequent starting, stopping and manoeuvring should be avoided, as should jerky movements and high sustained forces. The risk of injury is also increased if pushing or pulling is carried out with the hands much below waist height or above shoulder height. Being able to adopt a comfortable, stable posture is important and twisted or bent postures should be avoided.

96 Additionally, when pushing and pulling forces are transmitted from the handler's feet to the floor, the risk of slipping and consequent injury is much greater. For this reason, pushing or pulling a load in circumstances where the grip between foot and floor is poor – whether through the condition of the floor, footwear or both – is likely to increase the risk of injury significantly.

Does the task involve positioning the load precisely?

97 A requirement to position the load precisely may add to the risk of injury because:

(a) the load must be controlled into its final position and perhaps re-adjusted before it is put in place. This increases the effort and time required to complete the manual handling operation;

(b) it can involve more awkward postures.

Does the task involve a risk of sudden movement of the load?

98 If a load suddenly becomes free and the handler is unprepared or is not able to keep complete control of the load, unpredictable stresses can be imposed on the body, creating a risk of injury. For example, freeing a box jammed on a shelf or releasing a machine component during maintenance work can easily cause injury if handling conditions are not ideal. Problems may also occur during the handling of people or animals which may behave unpredictably. The risk is made worse if the handler's posture is unstable.

Does the task involve several risk factors?

99 Individual capability will be greatly reduced if twisting is combined with stooping or stretching. Such combinations should be avoided wherever possible, especially since their effect on individual capability can be worse than the simple addition of their individual effects might suggest.

24

Reducing the risk

Changing the task layout

100 There may be scope for changes to the layout of the task to reduce the risk of injury by, for example, improving the flow of materials or products. Such changes will often bring the additional benefits of increased efficiency and productivity. The optimum position for storage of loads, for example, is around waist height. Storage much above or below this height should be reserved for loads that are lighter, more easily handled, or handled infrequently.

Improving efficient use of the body

101 Changes to the task layout, the equipment used, or the sequence of operations can reduce or remove the need for twisting, stooping and stretching.

102 Generally, any change that allows the load to be held closer to the body is likely to reduce the risk of injury. The level of stress in the lower back will be reduced; the weight of the load will be more easily counterbalanced by the weight of the body; and the load will be more stable and the handler less likely to lose control of it. In addition, if the load is hugged to the body, friction with the handler's garments will steady it and may help to support its weight. The need for protective clothing should also be considered (see paragraphs 183-185).

103 When lifting of loads at or near floor level is unavoidable, take steps to eliminate or modify the task. If that is impossible then handling techniques which allow the use of the relatively strong leg muscles rather than those of the back are preferable, as long as the load is small enough to be held close to the trunk. In addition, if the task includes lifting to shoulder height, an intermediate step to allow the handler to change handgrip (see Figure 16) will help to reduce risk. Bear in mind, however, that such techniques impose heavy forces on the knees and hip joints which must carry both the weight of the load and the weight of the rest of the body.

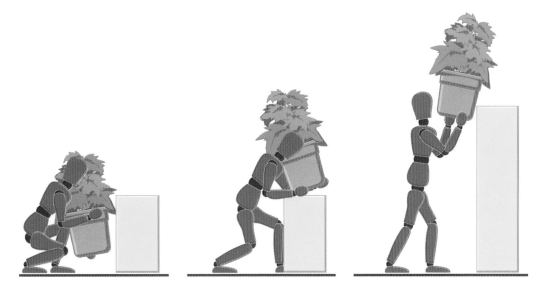

Figure 16 Use of midway stage to change grip

104 How close the load is positioned to the body can also be influenced by foot placement. Removing obstacles which need to be reached over or into – for example poorly placed pallets, excessively deep bins – will permit the handler's feet to be placed beneath or adjacent to the load (see Figure 17).

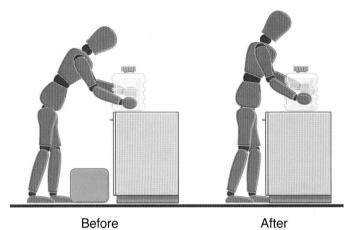

Before   After

Figure 17 Avoiding an obstructed lift. Organise the workplace so that the handler can get as close to the load as possible

105 Where possible the handler should be able to move in close to the load before beginning the manual handling operation. The handler should also be able to address the load squarely, preferably facing in the direction of intended movement.

106 The risk of injury may also be reduced if lifting can be replaced by controlled pushing or pulling. For example, it may be possible to slide the load or roll it along (see Figure 18). However, uncontrolled sliding or rolling, particularly of large or heavy loads, may introduce other risks of injury.

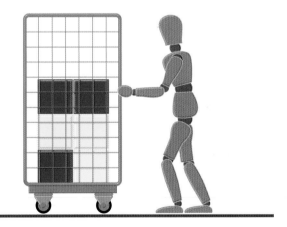

Figure 18 Hand position when pushing

107 For both pulling and pushing, a secure footing should be ensured, and the hands should not be applied to the load much below waist height or above shoulder height. A further option, where other safety considerations allow, is to push with the handler's back against the load (see Figure 19), using the strong leg muscles to exert the force.

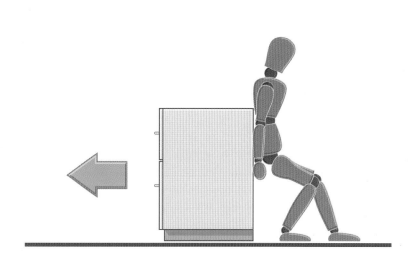

Figure 19 Using the strong leg muscles

Work routine

Does the task involve frequent or prolonged physical effort?

108   The frequency with which a load is handled can affect the risk of injury. A quite modest load, handled very frequently, can create as large a risk of injury as one-off handling of a heavier load. The effect will be worsened by jerky or hurried movements that can fatigue the body quickly.

109   If physical stresses are prolonged then fatigue will occur, for example of the muscles, increasing the risk of injury. This effect will often be made worse by a relatively fixed posture. The amount of work undertaken in fixed postures is an important consideration since blood flow to the muscles will be reduced, which leads to a rapid increase in fatigue and a corresponding fall in muscular efficiency.

110   The risk of manual handling injury can be reduced by careful attention to the work routine. Minimising the need for fixed postures due to prolonged holding or supporting of a load will reduce fatigue and the associated fall-off in muscular efficiency. Attention to the frequency of handling loads, especially those that are heavy or awkward, can also reduce fatigue and the risk of injury. Where possible, tasks should be self-paced and employees trained to adjust their rate of working to optimise safety and productivity.

Does the task involve insufficient rest or recovery periods?

111   Taking steps to reduce fatigue during physically demanding work decreases ill health and maintains output. It is important to ensure that there are adequate opportunities for rest (ie breaks from work) or recovery (ie changing to another task which uses a different set of muscles).

112   As there are large differences in how quickly individuals become fatigued, an inflexible provision of rest pauses may not be an efficient method of reducing the risk of injury. Mandatory, fixed breaks are generally less effective than those taken voluntarily within the constraints of what is possible in terms of work organisation.

113 A better solution can often be found in job rotation where this allows one group of muscles to rest while others are being used. Periods of heavy work may be interspersed with lighter activities such as paperwork or the monitoring of instruments. Job rotation can also bring advantages in reduced monotony and increased attentiveness. However, where rotation merely repeats the use of the same group of muscles, albeit on a different task, it is generally ineffective in reducing the risk of manual handling injury.

Does the task involve a rate of work imposed by a process?

114 Particular care is necessary where the worker cannot change the rate of work. Mild fatigue, which otherwise might quickly be relieved by a short pause or a brief spell doing another operation using different muscles, can soon become more pronounced, leading to an increased risk of injury.

Does the task involve handling while seated?

115 Handling loads while seated imposes considerable constraints. The relatively powerful leg muscles cannot be used. Nor can the weight of the handler's body be used as a counterbalance. Most of the work, therefore, has to be done by the weaker muscles of the arms and upper body.

116 Unless the load is presented close to the body the handler will have to reach and/or lean forward. Not only will handling in this position put the body under additional stress but the seat, unless firmly placed, will then tend to move as the handler attempts to maintain a stable posture. To prevent excessive twisting, loads should be lifted forwards from the body and not from the side. To reduce the load on the spine when lifting and to reduce the amount of undesirable movements, seats should be provided with an appropriate backrest.

117 Lifting from below the level of a work surface will almost inevitably result in twisting and stooping, the dangers of which were discussed in paragraphs 88 and 89.

118 The possibility of accidental movement of the seat should also be considered. Castors may be inadvisable, especially on hard floors. A swivel-action seat will help the handler to face the load without having to twist the trunk. The relative heights of seats and work surfaces should be well matched. Further advice on this is given in the HSE booklet *Seating at work*.[15]

Does the task involve team handling?

119 Handling by two or more people (see Figure 20) may make possible an operation that is beyond the capability of one person, or reduce the risk of injury to a single handler. However, team handling may introduce additional problems which the assessment should consider. During the handling operation the proportion of the load that is borne by each member of the team will inevitably vary to some extent. Such variation is likely to be more pronounced on sloping or uneven ground. Therefore, the load that a team can handle safely is less than the sum of the loads that the individual team members could cope with when working alone.

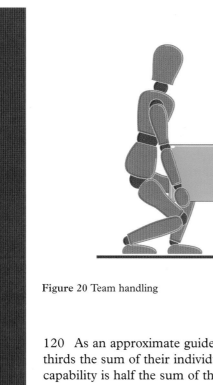

Figure 20 Team handling

120 As an approximate guide, the capability of a two-person team is two-thirds the sum of their individual capabilities and for a three-person team the capability is half the sum of their individual capabilities. Teams of more than four members are unlikely to work successfully. If steps or slopes must be negotiated, most of the weight may be borne by the handler or handlers at the lower end, further reducing the capability of the team as a whole.

121 There may be additional difficulties if:

(a) team members get in the way of each others' sight or movement; or

(b) the load does not have enough good handholds. This can occur particularly with compact loads which force the handlers to work close together or where the space available for movement is limited; or

(c) the background noise level is too high to allow easy communication between team members.

122 For safe team handling there should be enough space for the handlers to manoeuvre as a group. They should have adequate access to the load, and the load should provide sufficient handholds. If the load is particularly small or difficult to grasp, then a handling aid such as a stretcher or slings should be used. One person should plan and then take charge of the operation, ensuring that movements are co-ordinated. However, there should be good communication between team members.

123 When team handling is being carried out to handle a person, the person being handled should be included in the communication where possible. A clear protocol should be agreed between the team about timing for the lift. This is particularly necessary when the team contains employees from different agencies, for example, fire service and ambulance staff, who may have their own preferred instructions. Team members should preferably be of similar build and physical capability. Where the weight of the load is unevenly distributed, the strongest members of the team should take the heavier end.

The load

Size and weight

Is the load heavy?

124 The weight of a load is an important factor in assessing the risk from manual handling and for many years legislation and guidance on manual handling has concentrated on this. However, it is now well established that the weight of the load is only one – and sometimes not the main – consideration affecting the risk of injury. Other features of the load must also be considered, such as its:

(a) resistance to movement;

(b) size;

(c) shape; or

(d) rigidity.

125 The circumstances in which the load is handled must also be taken into account, for example:

(a) postural requirements;

(b) frequency and duration of handling;

(c) workplace design; and

(d) aspects of work organisation such as incentive schemes and piecework.

126 Also, traditional guidance, based on so-called 'acceptable' weights, has often considered only symmetrical, two-handed lifts, ie lifts that take place in front of and close to the body. In reality such lifting tasks are comparatively rare, since most will involve sideways movement, twisting of the trunk or some other asymmetry. For these reasons an approach to manual handling which concentrates only on the weight of the load is likely to be misleading, either failing adequately to deal with the risk of injury or imposing excessively cautious constraints.

127 The numerical guidelines and text in Appendix 3 consider the weight of the load in relation to other important factors, such as frequency of lift, twisting etc.

128 Where a risk of injury from a heavy load is identified, after taking into account the Appendix 3 guidelines and the points in paragraphs 124 and 125, consider reducing its weight. For example, materials like liquids and powders may be packaged in smaller containers. Where loads are bought in it may be possible to specify lower package weights. However, the breaking down of loads will not always be the safest course of action as this will increase the handling frequency. The effort associated with moving the handler's own body weight becomes more significant as the rate of handling rises. This can result in increased fatigue and excessive stresses on particular parts of the body, for example, the shoulders. Another option is to make the load so big that it cannot be handled manually.

129 If a variety of weights is to be handled, it may be possible to arrange the loads by weight so that additional precautions, for example lifting aids, can be used when handling the heaviest.

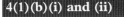

130 When moving and handling people, an individual risk assessment should be carried out and the result recorded. Typically this is located in their care plan. The care plan should accompany the patient wherever they go during treatment to ensure all staff involved with the care are aware of the requirements.

Is the load bulky or unwieldy?

131 The shape of a load will affect the way it can be held. For example, the risk of injury will be increased if a load to be lifted from the ground is not small enough to pass between the knees. In these circumstances, its size will prevent the worker getting close enough to pick it up safely. Similarly, if the bottom front corners of a load are not within reach when carried at waist height it will be harder to get a good grip. Also if handlers have to lean away from a load to keep it off the ground when carrying it at their side, they will be forced into unfavourable postures.

132 In general, if any dimension of the load exceeds about 75 cm, its handling is likely to pose an increased risk of injury, especially if this size is exceeded in more than one dimension. The risk will be further increased if the load does not provide convenient handholds. For loads of these dimensions, appropriate handling aids should be considered.

133 The bulk of the load can also interfere with vision. Where it is not possible to avoid a bulky load restricting a worker's vision then the increased risk of slipping, tripping, falling or colliding with obstructions should be taken into account. It may be possible to counteract this problem by considering a team lift. If one employee's vision is impeded by the load it may be possible for another employee to support the other end and therefore have a clear view.

134 The risk of injury will also be increased if the load is unwieldy and difficult to control. Well-balanced lifting may be difficult to achieve, the load may hit obstructions, or it may be affected by gusts of wind or other sudden air movements.

135 If the centre of gravity of the load is not positioned centrally within the load, inappropriate handling may increase the risk of injury. For example, loads which have much of the weight at the back should not be lifted from the front. This will place its centre of gravity further from the handler's body than if it is approached from the other side or is turned around and lifted from the back.

136 Sometimes, as with a sealed and unmarked package, an offset centre of gravity is not immediately apparent. In these circumstances, there is a greater risk of injury since the handler may unwittingly hold the load with its centre of gravity further from the body than is necessary.

Making the load easier to grasp

137 If the load is difficult to grasp, for example because it is large, rounded, smooth, wet or greasy, its handling will call for extra grip strength, which is tiring and will probably involve inadvertent changes of posture. There will also be a greater risk of dropping the load. Handling will be less easy and the risk of injury will be increased. Using gloves may also make a load more difficult to hold (see paragraph 185).

138 For awkward loads like this, consider providing handles, hand grips, indents or any other feature designed to improve the handler's grasp. Alternatively it may be possible to place the load securely in a container which

is easier to grasp. Where a load is bulky rather than heavy it may be easier to carry it at the side of the body, if it has suitable handholds. If not, slings or other carrying devices could be provided.

139 The positioning of handholds can help reduce the risk of injury. For example, handholds at the top of a load may reduce the temptation to stoop when lifting it from a low level. However, depending upon the size of the load, this might also mean carrying the load with bent arms which could increase fatigue.

140 Handholds should be wide enough to clear the width of the palm, and deep enough to accommodate the knuckles and any gloves which may need to be worn.

141 When pushing or pulling loads, a good hand grip or coupling with the load is essential. The load should be equipped with suitable hand grips, cut outs, or finger slots for two hands. The vertical height of the handle or handholds should be within the range of 91 to 114 cm. The handle or handholds should be of adequate length to allow variation in grasp for manoeuvring and manipulating the load. A handle diameter of 3.2 to 4.5 cm is recommended.

Making the load more stable

142 If the load is unstable, for example if it lacks rigidity or has contents that are liable to shift, the risk of injury is increased. The stresses arising during the manual handling of such a load are less predictable, and the instability may impose sudden additional stresses for which the handler is not prepared. This is particularly true if the handler is unfamiliar with a particular load and there is no cautionary marking on it.

143 Where possible any packaging should be designed to prevent the load from shifting unexpectedly while it is being handled. Ideally, containers holding liquids or free-moving powders should be well filled, leaving only a small amount of free space, as long as this does not increase the risk by increasing the weight significantly. Where this is not possible, consider alternative means of handling.

144 For non-rigid loads it may be advisable to use slings or other aids to keep control during handling.

Avoiding injuries from contact with the load

145 There may also be a risk of injury from contact with the load. It may have sharp edges or rough surfaces, or be too hot or too cold to touch safely without protective clothing. In addition to the more obvious risk of direct injury, such characteristics may also impair grip, discourage good posture or otherwise interfere with safe handling (see paragraphs 183-185).

146 As far as possible, loads should be clean and free from dust, oil, corrosive deposits etc. To prevent injury during the manual handling of hot or cold materials, an adequately insulated container should be used; if this is not possible, suitable handling aids or PPE will be necessary. Sharp corners, jagged edges, rough surfaces etc should be avoided where possible; again, where this cannot be achieved, the use of handling aids or PPE will be necessary. Further advice on selecting personal protective equipment is in paragraphs 183-185.

147 Handling animals which may react in an unpredictable way can increase the risk of injury.

Is the load being pushed or pulled?

148 For loads which are being pushed or pulled it is important to ensure that:

(a) the equipment being used is:

    (i) the correct type for the load involved;

    (ii) well maintained, particularly any braking system;

    (iii) fitted with the correct type of wheels, eg wheels that run easily over the surfaces involved;

    (iv) provided with the correct height handle;

(b) the load itself is:

    (i) stable and, if necessary, secured to the equipment being used to move it;

    (ii) not too bulky for the route or equipment being used;

    (iii) stacked, so that heavier items are at the bottom and it is possible to see over the load.

Designing equipment so it can be handled easily

149 The Supply of Machinery (Safety) Regulations 1992 (as amended)[16] cover the essential health and safety requirements in the design of machinery and its component parts. These Regulations require machinery to be capable of being handled safely. If manual handling is involved, the machinery and component parts must be easily movable or equipped for picking up, for example with hand grips. Machinery and component parts not suitable for manual handling must be fitted with attachments for lifting gear or designed so that standard lifting gear can be easily attached.

150 Regulation 10 of the Provision and Use of Work Equipment Regulations 1998 places duties on employers and they will need to check, for example, that adequate operating instructions have been provided and that there is information about residual risks such as manual handling. The employer should also check that:

(a) the equipment has no obvious faults or defects;

(b) the CE mark has been correctly applied; and

(c) an EC declaration of conformity is provided with the equipment.

151 For second-hand machinery the above does not apply (except if the machine has been substantially modified or where the machine is brought in from outside the European Union (EU) and has never been supplied from within the EU previously). However the HSW Act requires designers and manufacturers to ensure the safety, so far as is reasonably practicable, of any article for use at work and to provide adequate information about the conditions necessary to ensure that when put to use, such articles will be safe and without risk to health (see paragraph 175).

152 To ensure that adequate information is available for articles which are likely to cause injury if manually handled, it may be helpful to provide information on the weight. The simplest way of doing this is to mark the article with its weight. Alternatively, mark its package with the total weight prominently in a place or places where the handler will see it easily. For asymmetric articles likely to cause injury when lifted manually, the centre of gravity should be marked on the article or package.

The working environment

153 The issues dealt with in this section are also subject to the requirements of the Workplace (Health, Safety and Welfare) Regulations 1992.

Space constraints

Do the handlers have room to move around easily?

154 If the working environment hinders working at a safe height or the adoption of good posture, the risk of injury from manual handling will be increased. For example:

(a) low work surfaces or restricted headroom will result in the adoption of a stooping posture;

(b) furniture, fixtures or other obstructions may increase the need for twisting or leaning; and

(c) constricted working areas and narrow gangways will hinder the manoeuvring of bulky loads.

155 The provision of sufficient clear, well-maintained floor space and headroom in gangways and other working areas is important; constrictions caused by narrow doorways and the positioning of fixtures, machines etc should be avoided as far as possible. Allow adequate room for all the manoeuvres necessary during manual handling operations. In many cases, much can be achieved simply by improving the standard of housekeeping, for example by keeping workspaces clean and tidy.

156 Doors that are frequently used when moving loads should be opened automatically rather than manually (or wedged open until the task is finished). This can make carrying easier and will avoid the need to stop and start (which requires extra force) when pushing or pulling a load.

Nature and condition of floors

Are there uneven, slippery or unstable floors?

157 On permanent sites, both indoors and out, a flat, well-maintained and properly drained surface should be provided. In construction, agriculture and other activities where manual handling may take place on temporary surfaces, the ground should be prepared if possible and kept even and firm; if possible, suitable coverings should be provided. Temporary work platforms should be firm and stable.

158 Spillages of water, oil, soap, food scraps and other substances likely to make the floor slippery should be cleared away promptly. Slip-resistant surfaces should be considered if floors are likely to become wet or slippery.

34

159　In addition to increasing the likelihood of slips, trips and falls, uneven or slippery floors hinder smooth movement and create additional unpredictability. Unstable footrests and floors susceptible to movement, for example, on a boat, a moving train, or a mobile work platform, similarly increase the risk of injury through the imposition of sudden, unpredictable stresses. In these conditions, the capability to handle loads in safety may be reduced significantly.

160　When pushing and pulling loads, floor or ground surfaces should be level, clean, dry and unbroken. Slopes or ramps should be low gradient. For pushing and pulling loads on uneven surfaces the force required to start the load moving could increase by as much as 10%.

Working at different levels

Are there variations in floor level?

161　The presence of steps, steep slopes etc can increase the risk of injury by making movement more difficult when handling loads. Carrying a load up or down a ladder, if it cannot be avoided, is likely to make handling problems worse because of the need to keep a hold on the ladder.

162　Where possible, all manual handling activities should be carried out on a single level. Where more than one level is involved, the transition should preferably be made by a gentle slope or, failing that, by well-positioned and properly maintained steps. Manual handling on steep slopes should be avoided as far as possible.

163　The presence of slopes is an important consideration when pushing or pulling loads. Pushing is generally preferable to pulling. Slopes should not be so steep as to make keeping control of the load difficult.

164　Another risk from pushing/pulling on a slope is that the forces involved are increased. For example, for a load of 400 kg and a slope of 1 in 12 (4.8°), the additional force required is 33 kg (330 newtons). This is above the guideline weight for males and well in excess of the guideline weight for females. Table 2 shows the approximate increase in push forces that can be expected per 100 kg of load, on different slope angles.

Table 2 Effect of slope angle on push force

Slope gradient (degrees)	Push force (kg) increase per 100 kg of laden trolley weight
1	2
3	5
5	9
7	12
10	17.5

Are work surfaces at different heights?

165　Too much variation between the heights of working surfaces, storage shelving etc will increase the range of movement and therefore the risk of injury. This is particularly so if the variation is large and requires, for example, movement of the load from near floor level to shoulder height or higher.

Therefore it is good practice to provide either:

(a) working surfaces, such as benches, that are at a uniform height to reduce the need for raising or lowering loads; or

(b) height-adjustable equipment, for example a scissor lift.

Thermal environment and ventilation

Are there extremes of temperature, high humidity or gusts of wind that may affect handling?

166 The risk of injury during manual handling will be increased by extreme thermal conditions. For example, high temperatures or humidity can cause rapid fatigue and perspiration on the hands may reduce grip. Work at low temperatures may impair dexterity. Any gloves and other protective clothing which may be necessary may also hinder movement, impair dexterity and reduce grip. The influence of air movement on working temperatures – the wind chill factor – should also be considered.

167 To provide a comfortable work environment for manual handling, extremes of temperature, excessive humidity and poor ventilation should be avoided where possible. This can be done either by improving environmental control or relocating the work.

168 Where these conditions cannot be changed, for example when manual handling has to be done out of doors in extreme weather, or close to a very hot process, or in a refrigerated storage area, the use of PPE will be necessary. The advice given in paragraphs 183-185 should be followed.

Strong air movements and gusts of wind

169 Inadequate ventilation can hasten fatigue, increasing the risk of injury. Sudden air movements, whether caused by a ventilation system or the wind, can make large loads more difficult to manage safely.

Lighting

Are there poor lighting conditions?

170 Poor lighting conditions can increase the risk of injury. Dimness or glare may cause poor posture, for example by encouraging stooping. Contrast between areas of bright light and deep shadow can aggravate tripping hazards and hinder the accurate judgement of height and distance.

171 There should be sufficient well-directed light to enable handlers to see clearly what they are doing and the layout of the workplace, and to make accurate judgements of distance and position.

Information on the load

172 Regulation 4(1)(b)(iii) can be complied with in a variety of ways, depending on the circumstances.

173 The requirement to provide 'general indications' of the weight and nature of the loads to be handled should form part of any basic training, so that employees have sufficient information to carry out the operations they are likely to be asked to do.

Guidance

4(1)(b)(iii)

174 Where it is reasonably practicable, employers should give precise information. For employers whose businesses originate loads (manufacturers, packers etc) the simplest way of providing this information is by marking it on the loads.

175 The Regulations impose duties on employers whose employees carry out manual handling. However, those who originate loads that are likely to undergo manual handling may also have relevant duties, for example under sections 3 or 6 of the HSW Act, for the health and safety of other people at work. They should make loads as easy to grasp and handle as possible, and mark loads clearly with their weight and, where appropriate, an indication of their heaviest side (see paragraphs 149-152).

Regulation

4(2)

(2)   Any assessment such as is referred to in paragraph (1)(b)(i) of this regulation shall be reviewed by the employer who made it if –

(a)   there is reason to suspect that it is no longer valid; or

(b)   there has been a significant change in the manual handling operations to which it relates;

and where as a result of any such review changes to an assessment are required, the relevant employer shall make them.

Guidance

4(2)

Reviewing the assessment

176 The assessment should be kept up to date. It should be reviewed if new information comes to light or if there has been a change in the manual handling operations. The assessment should also be reviewed if a reportable injury occurs or when individual employees suffer an illness, injury or the onset of disability which may make them more vulnerable to risk.

Regulation

4(3)

(3)   In determining for the purposes of this regulation whether manual handling operations at work involve a risk of injury and in determining the appropriate steps to reduce that risk regard shall be had in particular to:

(a)   the physical suitability of the employee to carry out the operations;

(b)   the clothing, footwear or other personal effects he is wearing;

(c)   his knowledge and training;

(d)   the results of any relevant risk assessment carried out pursuant to regulation 3 of the Management of Health and Safety at Work Regulations 1999;

(e)   whether the employee is within a group of employees identified by that assessment as being especially at risk; and

(f)   the results of any health surveillance provided pursuant to regulation 6 of the Management of Health and Safety at Work Regulations 1999.

Guidance

4(3)(a)

Individual capability

Physical suitability of the employee

Does the task require unusual strength, height etc?

177 The ability to carry out manual handling safely varies between individuals. These variations, however, are less important than the nature of

the handling operations in causing manual handling injuries. Assessments which concentrate on individual capability at the expense of task or workplace design are likely to be misleading. (Employers should also be aware of their duties under the Disability Discrimination Act 1995,[17] particularly section 6.)

178 In general the lifting strength of women is less than that of men. But for both men and women the range of individual strength and ability is large, and there is considerable overlap – some women can safely handle greater loads than some men.

179 An individual's physical capability varies with age, typically climbing until the early twenties and then gradually declining. This decline becomes more significant from the mid-forties. The risk of manual handling injury may therefore be slightly higher for employees in their teens or those in their fifties and sixties. Particular care is needed in the design of tasks for these groups who are more likely to be working close to their maximum capacity in manual handling. Also, older workers may tire more quickly and will take longer to recover from musculoskeletal injury. However, the range of individual capability is large and the benefits of experience and maturity should not be overlooked.

180 An employee's manual handling capability can be affected by their health status, for example care needs to be taken when considering placing an individual with a history of back pain in a job which involves heavy manual handling. In cases of doubt, the help of an occupational health professional should be sought. However, individuals should not be excluded from work unless there is a good medical reason for restricting their activity. Special consideration should also be given to new and expectant mothers whose capabilities may be affected by hormonal changes. Further advice on this is in HSG122 *New and expectant mothers at work: A guide for employers*[18] (see also paragraphs 205-206).

181 The nature of the work needs to be considered when deciding whether the physical demands imposed by manual handling operations should be regarded as unusual. For example, demands that would be considered unusual for a group of employees engaged in office work might not be out of the ordinary for those normally involved in heavy physical labour. It would also be unrealistic to ignore the element of self-selection that often occurs for jobs that are relatively demanding physically.

182 As a general rule, however, the risk of injury should be regarded as unacceptable if the manual handling operations cannot be performed satisfactorily by most reasonably fit, healthy employees.

Clothing, footwear or other personal effects

Personal protective equipment and other clothing

183 Personal protective equipment (PPE) should be used only as a last resort, when engineering or other controls do not provide adequate protection. If wearing PPE cannot be avoided, its implications for the risk of manual handling injury should be considered. For example, gloves may make gripping difficult and the weight of gas cylinders used with breathing apparatus will increase the stresses on the body. Some clothing, such as a uniform, may restrict movement during manual handling (see the Personal Protective Equipment at Work Regulations 1992, as amended).[19]

184 However, where the use of PPE is necessary, the protection that it offers should not be compromised to make the manual handling operations easier.

Alternative methods of handling may be necessary where the manual handling is likely to lead to risks from the contents of the load or from contamination on the outside of the load.

185 All work clothing, including any PPE, should be well-fitting and restrict movement as little as possible. Fasteners, pockets and other features on which loads might snag should be concealed. Gloves should be close-fitting and supple, so that they don't make gripping difficult. Footwear should provide adequate support, a stable, non-slip base and proper protection. Restrictions on the handler's movement caused by wearing protective clothing need to be recognised in the design of the task.

Abdominal and back support belts

186 There are many different types of abdominal and back support belts which are claimed to be lifting aids. They may help reduce the effect of the physical demands of the task and so reduce the risk of injury to the handler. There is currently no conclusive evidence which supports these claims and some studies show that they have no effect on injury rates. Some evidence suggests that wearing a belt may make particular individuals more susceptible to injury or to more severe injury. Also they may have long-term effects, with prolonged use, such as a weakening of support muscles. The effectiveness of back belts to reduce risk, therefore, remains controversial.

187 It will normally be preferable to reduce the risk more directly and effectively, therefore, through safer systems of working. These could incorporate engineering, design or organisation changes to alter features concerned with the task, load or the working environment. Such measures will provide protection for the whole group of workers involved rather than to individual workers.

4(3)(b)

Knowledge and training

Is special information or training needed to enable the task to be done safely?

188 Section 2 of the HSW Act and regulations 10 and 13 of the Management Regulations require employers to provide their employees with health and safety information and training. This should be supplemented as necessary with more specific information and training on manual handling injury risks and prevention, as part of the steps to reduce risk required by regulation 4(1)(b)(ii) of the Regulations.

189 The risk of injury from a manual handling task will be increased where workers do not have the information or training necessary to enable them to work safely. For example, if they do not know about any unusual characteristics of loads or about the system of work designed to ensure their safety during manual handling, this may lead to injury. It is essential that where, for example, mechanical handling aids are available, training is provided in their proper use.

190 The provision of information and training alone will not ensure safe manual handling. The first objective in reducing the risk of injury should always be to design the manual handing operations to be as safe as is reasonably practicable. This will involve improving the task, the working environment and reducing the load weight as appropriate. Where possible the manual handling operations should be designed to suit individuals, not the other way round. Effective training will complement a safe system of work, and has an important part to play in reducing the risk of manual handling injury. It is not a substitute for a safe system of work.

4(3)(c)

191 Employers should make sure that their employees understand clearly how manual handling operations have been designed to ensure their safety. Employees, their safety representatives and safety committees should be involved in developing and implementing manual handling training and monitoring its effectiveness. This will include, for example, checking that any training is actually being put into practice and that accident rates have reduced. As with assessors, if in-house personnel are used to act as trainers, suitable checks should be made to ensure that they have understood the information given to them and have reached an adequate level of competence.

192 HSE does not publish prescriptive guidance on what a 'good' manual handling training course should include or how long it should last. However, in general, courses should be suitable for the individual, tasks and environment involved, use relevant examples and last long enough to cover all the relevant information. Such information is likely to include advice on:

(a) manual handling risk factors and how injuries can occur;

(b) how to carry out safe manual handling, including good handling technique (see paragraphs 197-198);

(c) appropriate systems of work for the individual's task and environment;

(d) use of mechanical aids; and

(e) practical work to allow the trainer to identify and put right anything the trainee is not doing safely.

193 Employers should ensure they keep sufficient records to show who has been trained, when the training was carried out and what the content of the course was. Employers should establish a planned training programme to ensure all staff identified as requiring it receive basic training with updates as required. This programme should also cover new starters to try to ensure training takes place either before or as close to starting a new job as possible. Managers may also wish to monitor sickness absence and near-miss reporting as one way to assess the efficacy of the training.

194 Employees should be trained to recognise loads whose weight, in conjunction with their shape and other features, and the circumstances in which they are handled, might cause injury. Simple methods for estimating weight on the basis of volume may be taught. Where volume is less important than the density of the contents, as, for example, in the case of a dustbin containing refuse, an alternative technique for assessing the safety of handling should be taught, such as rocking the load from side to side before attempting to lift it (see Figure 21).

195 In general, unfamiliar loads should be treated with caution. For example, it should not be assumed that apparently empty drums or other closed containers are actually empty. They should be tested first, for example by trying to raise one end. Employees should be taught to apply force gradually until either too much strain is felt, in which case the task should be reconsidered, or it is apparent that the task is within the handler's capability.

196 When workers are given appropriate training, it is important to ensure that supervisors and other more senior staff are also aware of the good practices that have been recommended, and that they regularly encourage the workforce to adopt appropriate techniques and ensure they continue to be used.

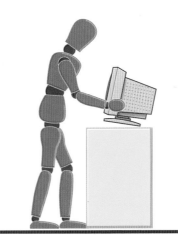

Figure 21 Rocking a load to assess its ease of handling

Good handling technique

197   A good handling technique is no substitute for other risk-reduction steps, such as provision of lifting aids, or improvements to the task, load or working environment. Moving the load by rocking, pivoting, rolling or sliding is preferable to lifting it in situations where scope for risk reduction is limited. However, good handling technique forms a very valuable addition to other risk-control measures. To be successful, good handling technique demands both training and practice. The training should be carried out in conditions that are as realistic as possible, emphasising its relevance to everyday handling operations.

198   There is no single correct way to lift and many different approaches are put forward. Each has merits and advantages in particular situations or individual circumstances. The content of training in good handling technique should be tailored to the particular handling operations likely to be undertaken. It should begin with relatively simple examples and progress to more specialised handling operations as appropriate. The following list, based on research carried out for HSE by the Institute of Occupational Medicine,[20] illustrates some important points which are relevant to a two-handed symmetrical lift, ie a lift using both hands that takes place in front of and close to the body:

(a)   **Think before handling/lifting.** Plan the lift/handling activity. Where is the load going to be placed? Use appropriate handling aids where possible. Will help be needed with the load? Remove obstructions, such as discarded wrapping materials. For long lifts, such as from floor to shoulder height, consider resting the load mid-way on a table or bench to change grip.

(b) **Keep the load close to the waist.** Keep the load close to the waist for as long as possible while lifting. The distance of the load from the spine at waist height is an important factor in the overall load on the spine and back muscles. Keep the heaviest side of the load next to the body. If a close approach to the load is not possible, try to slide it towards the body before attempting to lift it.

(c) **Adopt a stable position.** The feet should be apart with one leg slightly forward to maintain balance (alongside the load if it is on the ground). The worker should be prepared to move their feet during the lift to maintain a stable posture. Wearing over-tight clothing or unsuitable footwear may make this difficult.

(d) **Ensure a good hold on the load.** Where possible hug the load as close as possible to the body. This may be better than gripping it tightly only with the hands.

(e) **Moderate flexion (slight bending) of the back, hips and knees at the start of the lift** is preferable to either fully flexing the back (stooping) or fully flexing the hips and knees (full/deep squatting).

(f) **Don't flex the back any further while lifting.** This can happen if the legs begin to straighten before starting to raise the load.

(g) **Avoid twisting the back or leaning sideways especially while the back is bent.** Keep shoulders level and facing in the same direction as the hips. Turning by moving the feet is better than twisting and lifting at the same time.

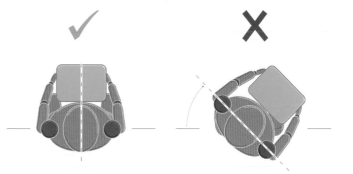

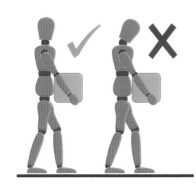

(h) **Keep the head up when handling.** Look ahead, not down at the load once it has been held securely.

(i) **Move smoothly.** Do not jerk or snatch the load as this can make it harder to keep control and can increase the risk of injury.

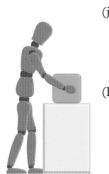

(j) **Don't lift or handle more than can be easily managed.** There is a difference between what people can lift and what they can safely lift. If in doubt, seek advice or get help.

(k) **Put down, then adjust**. If precise positioning of the load is necessary, put it down first, then slide it into the desired position.

Figure 22 Basic lifting operations

Vocational qualifications

199 The development of specific statements of what needs to be done, how well and by whom (ie statements of competence) will help to determine the extent of any shortfall in training. Such statements may be embodied in qualifications accredited by the National Council for Vocational Qualifications (NCVQ) and SCOTVEC (the Scottish Vocational Education Council).

Risk assessment findings

200 In deciding if there is a risk of injury, employers have to take account of the results of any relevant risk assessments under the Management Regulations. Relevant findings might include, for example:

(a) the results of specific risk assessments for young people or new and expectant mothers;

(b) particular aspects of workplace layout; or

(c) work organisation.

201 Employees should be informed of any relevant findings relating to the risks from manual handling which have been identified by the risk assessment.

Employees especially at risk

202 Particular consideration should be given to employees who:

(a) are or have recently been pregnant; or

(b) are known to have a history of back, knee or hip trouble, hernia or other health problems which could affect their manual handling capability; or

(c) have previously had a manual handling injury; or

(d) are young workers.

203 Clearly an individual's state of health, fitness and strength can significantly affect their ability to perform a task safely. But even though these characteristics vary enormously, studies have not shown any close correlation between any of them and injury incidence. There is, therefore, insufficient evidence for reliable selection of individuals for safe manual handling on the basis of such criteria. It is recognised, however, that there is often a degree of self-selection for work that is physically demanding.

204 It is also recognised that motivation and self-confidence in the ability to handle loads are important factors in reducing the risk of injury. These are linked with fitness and familiarity. Unaccustomed exertion – whether in a new task or on return from holiday or sickness absence – can carry a significant risk of injury and requires particular care.

205 Allowance should be made for pregnancy where the employer could reasonably be expected to be aware of it, ie where the pregnancy is visibly apparent or the employee has informed her employer that she is pregnant. Manual handling has significant implications for the health of the pregnant worker (and the foetus), particularly if combined with long periods of standing and/or walking. Hormonal changes during pregnancy can affect the ligaments and joints increasing the risk of injury during the last three months. As pregnancy progresses it also becomes more difficult to achieve and maintain good postures and this further reduces manual handling capability. Particular care should also be taken for women who may handle loads during the three months following a return to work after childbirth (further advice is contained in HSG122 *New and expectant mothers at work*).

206 When an employee informs her employer that she is pregnant, the risks to the health and safety of the worker and her unborn child must be assessed in accordance with the duties under the Management Regulations. A useful way to ensure compliance and make certain that workers can continue to work safely during pregnancy is to have a well-defined plan on how to respond when pregnancy is confirmed. Such a plan may include:

(a) re-assessment of the handling task (positioning of the load and feet, frequency of lifting) to consider what improvements might be made;

(b) training in recognising ways in which the work may be altered to help with changes in posture and physical capability, including the timing and frequency of rest periods;

(c) consideration of job-sharing, relocation or suspension on full pay where the risk cannot be reduced by a change to the working conditions;

(d) liaison with the GP to confirm that the pregnant worker is capable of performing work duties; and

(e) careful monitoring of the employees returning to work following childbirth to assess the need for changes to work organisation.

207 The Disability Discrimination Act 1995 places a duty on employers (currently those employing 15 or more, but as from October 2004 all employers) to make reasonable adjustments to the workplace or employment arrangements so that a disabled person is not at any substantial disadvantage compared to a non-disabled person. This might include, for example, arranging to limit the number, size or weight of loads handled by someone with a disability that limits their manual handling ability. Further guidance is given in the Department of Work and Pensions *Code of practice for the elimination of discrimination in the field of employment against disabled persons or persons who have had a disability.*[21]

208 Allowance should also be made for any health problem of which the employer could reasonably be expected to be aware and which might have a bearing on the ability to carry out manual handling operations in safety. If there is good reason to suspect that an individual's state of health might significantly increase the risk of injury from manual handling operations, seek medical advice.

Health surveillance

209 Health surveillance is putting into place systematic, regular and appropriate procedures to detect early signs of work-related ill health among employees exposed to certain health risks and acting on the results.

210 There is no duty in the Regulations to carry out health surveillance. Paragraph 41 of the Approved Code of Practice on the Management Regulations requires appropriate health surveillance to be carried out when certain criteria are met. However, one of these is that there are valid techniques available to detect indications of the disease or condition. Currently no techniques are available that would reliably detect early indications of ill health caused by manual handling and there is therefore no requirement for health surveillance to be carried out.

211 Nevertheless valuable information can be obtained from less precise measures such as reporting, monitoring and investigation of symptoms. This is known as 'health monitoring'. It is good practice to put in place systems that allow individuals to make early reports of manual handling injuries or back pain. Where appropriate these can be supplemented, for example by monitoring sickness absence records, lifestyle and health promotions and annual health checks. Further advice is in HSG61 *Health surveillance at work.*[22]

Regulation 5

Duty of employees

Each employee while at work shall make full and proper use of any system of work provided for his use by his employer in compliance with regulation 4(1)(b)(ii) of these Regulations.

212 Duties are already placed on employees by section 7 of the HSW Act under which they must:

(a) take reasonable care for their own health and safety and that of others who may be affected by their activities; and

(b)   co-operate with their employers to enable them to comply with their health and safety duties.

213   In addition, regulation 14 of the Management Regulations requires employees generally to make use of appropriate equipment provided for them, in accordance with their training and the instructions their employer has given them. Such equipment will include machinery and other aids provided for the safe handling of loads.

214   Regulation 5 of the Manual Handling Operations Regulations supplements these general duties in the case of manual handling. It requires employees to follow appropriate systems of work laid down by their employer to promote safety during the handling of loads.

Emergency action

215   These provisions do not preclude well-intentioned improvisation in an emergency, for example during efforts to rescue a casualty, fight a fire or contain a dangerous spillage.

Regulation 6

Regulation

6

Exemption certificates

(1)   The Secretary of State for Defence may, in the interests of national security, by a certificate in writing exempt –

(a)   any of the home forces, any visiting force or any headquarters from any requirement imposed by regulation 4 of these Regulations; or

(b)   any member of the home forces, any member of a visiting force or any member of a headquarters from the requirement imposed by regulation 5 of these Regulations;

and any exemption such as is specified in sub-paragraph (a) or (b) of this paragraph may be granted subject to conditions and to a limit of time and may be revoked by the said Secretary of State by a further certificate in writing at any time.

(2)   In this regulation –

(a)   "the home forces" has the same meaning as in section 12(1) of the Visiting Forces Act 1952;[(a)]

(b)   "headquarters" has the same meaning as in article 3(2) of the Visiting Forces and International Headquarters (Application of Law) Order 1965;[(b)]

(c)   "member of a headquarters" has the same meaning as in paragraph 1(1) of the Schedule to the International Headquarters and Defence Organisations Act 1964;[(c)] and

(d)   "visiting force" has the same meaning as it does for the purposes of any provision of Part I of the Visiting Forces Act 1952.

(a) 1952 c.67.
(b) SI 1965/1536 This has now been replaced by the 1999 Order of the same name (1999/1736); headquarters to which the Order applies are now listed in Schedule 2 of that instrument.
(c) 1964 c.5.

Regulation 7   Extension outside Great Britain

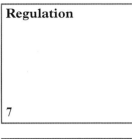

These Regulations shall, subject to regulation 3 hereof, apply to and in relation to the premises and activities outside Great Britain to which sections 1 to 59 and 80 to 82 of the Health and Safety at Work etc Act 1974 apply by virtue of the Health and Safety at Work etc Act 1974 (Application Outside Great Britain) Order 1989(d) as they apply within Great Britain.

(d) SI 1989/840.

216   The Regulations apply to offshore activities covered by the 2001 Order (the replacement for the 1989 order now in force) on or associated with oil and gas installations, including mobile installations, diving support vessels, heavy lift barges and pipe-lay barges.

Regulation 8   Repeals and revocations

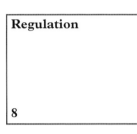

(1)   The enactments mentioned in column 1 of Part I of Schedule 2 to these Regulations are repealed to the extent specified in the corresponding entry in column 3 of that part.

(2)   The Regulations mentioned in column 1 of Part II of Schedule 2 to these Regulations are revoked to the extent specified in the corresponding entry in column 3 of that part.

217   The Regulations, like the European Directive on manual handling, apply a modern ergonomic approach to the prevention of injury. They take account of a wide range of relevant factors, including the nature of the task, the load, the working environment and individual capability. The Regulations have, therefore, replaced a number of outdated provisions which concentrated on the weight of the load being handled. The provisions are listed in Schedule 2 to the Regulations (not reproduced in this document).

Schedule 1

Factors to which the employer must have regard and questions he must consider when making an assessment of manual handling operations

Schedule 1

Regulation 4(1)(b)(i)

Column 1	Column 2
Factors	*Questions*
1 The tasks	Do they involve:
	- holding or manipulating loads at distance from trunk?
	- unsatisfactory bodily movement or posture, especially:
	- twisting the trunk?
	- stooping?
	- reaching upwards?
	- excessive movement of loads, especially:
	- excessive lifting or lowering distances?
	- excessive carrying distances?
	- excessive pushing or pulling of loads?
	- risk of sudden movement of loads?
	- frequent or prolonged physical effort?
	- insufficient rest or recovery periods?
	- a rate of work imposed by a process?
2 The loads	Are they:
	- heavy?
	- bulky or unwieldy?
	- difficult to grasp?
	- unstable, or with contents likely to shift?
	- sharp, hot or otherwise potentially damaging?
3 The working environment	Are there:
	- space constraints preventing good posture?
	- uneven, slippery or unstable floors?
	- variations in level of floors or work surfaces?
	- extremes of temperature or humidity?

48

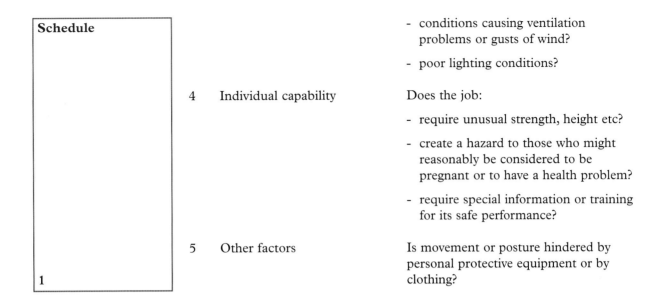

Schedule

1

4   Individual capability

5   Other factors

- conditions causing ventilation problems or gusts of wind?

- poor lighting conditions?

Does the job:

- require unusual strength, height etc?

- create a hazard to those who might reasonably be considered to be pregnant or to have a health problem?

- require special information or training for its safe performance?

Is movement or posture hindered by personal protective equipment or by clothing?

Appendix 1

Principles of a successful risk control/management system for controlling the risks from manual handling

1   Compliance with the Regulations by following the advice in this booklet will go a long way towards controlling the risks from manual handling. However, it is good practice to continue monitoring levels of sickness absence and discomfort due to manual handling injuries as a check that risk control is, and continues to be, successful.

2   There may be some instances where injury is still occurring and more steps are needed to tackle the problem. HSE recommends a seven-stage approach to controlling risks from musculoskeletal disorders. The stages needed are:

(a)   understand the issues and commit to action:

    (i)   are the risks from manual handling recognised in your workplace?

    (ii)   is management committed to preventing or minimising these risks?

    (iii) are there adequate management systems or policies to support the commitment?

(b)   create the right organisational environment:

    (i)   is worker participation actively sought and valued, for example is there active participation in risk assessment, selection of controls and subsequent reviews?

    (ii)   are safety representatives involved?

    (iii) are all departments aware of the contributions they can make?

    (iv)   is competence ensured?

    (v)   have you allocated responsibilities?

(c)   assess the risks from manual handling in your workplace:

    (i)   are manual handling risk factors present? For example, twisting, stooping, reaching, carrying heavy loads, slippery floors.

(d)   avoid or, where this is not possible, reduce the risks from manual handling:

    (i)   have you used an ergonomic approach? (See paragraph 13 of the main document.)

    (ii)   have you looked for 'higher order' solutions, ie can you avoid the manual handling altogether? If not, can you, for example, mechanise/automate, provide handling aids, reduce the weight of the load?

    (iii) have you prioritised your actions to control the risks from manual handling?

    (iv)   have you implemented solutions?

(v) have you reviewed their effectiveness?

(e) educate, inform and consult your workforce:

(i) have you consulted safety representatives/other workers and involved them in the risk assessment process?

(ii) have you educated and informed your workforce to enable them to play an active part in controlling risk?

(iii) what steps have you taken to ensure that training reinforces safe working practices and control measures?

(f) manage any case of manual handling injury:

(i) have you implemented and supported a system for early reporting of manual handling injuries and investigating which work activities could be linked with the symptoms?

(ii) do you actively look for symptoms of manual handling injury?

(iii) have you arranged for occupational health provision?

(iv) do you have systems in place for employees returning to work after having a manual handling injury, including a review of the risk assessment in light of their individual needs?

(g) carry out regular checks on programme effectiveness:

(i) do you have systems in place to monitor and review your controls for reducing the risks from manual handling?

(ii) do you have systems in place to monitor and review your manual handling management programme?

(iii) are you aware of new developments/information?

(iv) do you aim for continuous improvement?

3   Adequate control of risk factors will go a long way to prevent the occurrence of ill health caused by manual handling. Due to individual differences it is not possible to ensure that every possible manual handling injury will always be prevented. It is therefore important that employers should have a system in place to detect and manage any cases of work-related manual handling injury. Such systems should:

(a) encourage the early reporting of any symptoms. An individual's willingness to do this varies, so it is important to establish a supportive climate in the workplace that emphasises the benefits of early detection of possible harm;

(b) provide appropriate advice for users who report symptoms;

(c) provide for referral to health professionals to obtain appropriate diagnosis, treatment, or advice; and

(d) help employees who report symptoms to continue working, or to return to work after periods of absence or treatment. Rehabilitation must be supported by graduated return to work schemes.

Appendix 2   Assessment of manual handling risks - overview

1   The Regulations set no specific requirements such as weight limits. Instead, they focus on the needs of the individual and set out a hierarchy of measures to be implemented to ensure worker safety during manual handling operations. These measures are:

(a)   avoid hazardous manual handling operations so far as is reasonably practicable;

(b)   make a suitable and sufficient assessment of any hazardous manual handling operations that cannot be avoided; and

(c)   reduce the risk of injury from those operations so far as is reasonably practicable.

2   Where manual handling operations cannot be avoided, employers have a duty to make a suitable and sufficient assessment of the risks to health. This assessment must take into account the range of relevant factors listed in Schedule 1 to the Regulations.

3   HSE has developed the following three aids to risk assessment:

(a)   a risk assessment filter (Appendix 3). This is often a good starting point, as it is intended to save effort by screening out straightforward low-risk cases. A detailed assessment of every manual handling operation would be a major undertaking, and many handling operations, for example the occasional lifting of a small lightweight object, will involve negligible handling risk;

(b)   risk assessment checklists (Appendix 4) for use in cases where a full assessment is needed;

(c)   a manual handling assessment chart (MAC) (Appendix 5). This is an optional tool, which is still under development, which can be used as part of making a full risk assessment. In situations where it is applicable, it can help with quick identification of high-risk activities. The MAC does not cover all of the risk factors, and so only forms a part of the assessment process.

Factors to consider

4   The following physical risk factors are discussed in detail in the main body of this document: the task, the load, the working environment and individual capability. However, to ensure that all potential risk factors have been included in the assessment, then psychosocial (work organisation) factors should also be considered.

5   Psychosocial risk factors are things that may affect workers' psychological response to their work and workplace conditions (including working relationships with supervisors and colleagues). Examples are:

(a)   high workloads;

(b)   tight deadlines;

(c)   lack of control of the work and working methods.

6   As well as leading to stress, which is a hazard in its own right, psychosocial risk factors can contribute to the onset of musculoskeletal disorders. For example, there can be stress-related changes in the body (such as increased muscle tension) that can make people more susceptible to musculoskeletal problems; or individuals may change their behaviour, for example doing without rest breaks to try and cope with deadlines.

7   So both the physical and psychosocial factors need to be identified and controlled to have the greatest benefit. The best way to achieve this is by using an ergonomic approach, which looks at achieving the best 'fit' between the work, the working environment and the needs and capabilities of the workers.

8   Many jobs are not well designed and may include some or all of the following undesirable features, which may in turn lead to psychosocial risks:

(a)   workers have little control over their work and work methods (including shift patterns);

(b)   workers are unable to make full use of their skills;

(c)   workers, as a rule, are not involved in making decisions that affect them;

(d)   workers are expected to only carry out repetitive, monotonous tasks;

(e)   work is machine or system paced (and may be monitored inappropriately);

(f)   work demands are perceived as excessive;

(g)   payment systems encourage working too quickly or without breaks.

What can I do to reduce the risks of psychosocial factors?

9   As with physical risk factors, psychosocial factors are best addressed with full consultation and involvement of the workforce. Consider the following control measures that can often be applied to improve the working environment within your workplace:

(a)   reducing the monotony of tasks where appropriate;

(b)   ensuring there are reasonable workload (neither too much or too little) deadlines and demands;

(c)   ensuring good communication and reporting of problems;

(d)   encouraging teamwork;

(e)   monitoring and control of shift work or overtime working;

(f)   reducing or monitoring payment systems which work on piece rate;

(g)   providing appropriate training.

Appendix 3   Risk assessment filter

1   The filter described in this Appendix is relevant to:

(a)   lifting and lowering;

(b)   carrying for short distances;

(c)   pushing and pulling; and

(d)   handling while seated.

2   It is most likely to be useful if you think that the activity to be assessed is low risk - the filter should quickly and easily confirm (or deny) this. If using the filter shows the risk is within the guidelines, you do not normally have to do any other form of risk assessment unless you have individual employees who may be at significant risk, for example pregnant workers, young workers, those with a significant health problem or a recent manual handling injury. However these filter guidelines only apply when the load is easy to grasp and held in a good working environment.

3   However, the filter is less likely to be useful if:

(a)   there is a strong chance the work activities to be assessed involve significant risks from manual handling; or

(b)   the activities are complex. The use of the filter will only be worthwhile if it is possible to quickly (say within ten minutes) assess whether the guidelines in it are exceeded.

4   In either of these cases using the filter may not save any time or effort, so it may be better to opt immediately for the more detailed risk assessment in Appendix 4.

5   The filter is based partly on data in published scientific literature and partly on accumulated practical experience of assessing risks from manual handling. Its guideline figures are pragmatic, tried and tested; they are not based on any precise scientific formulae. The intention is to set out an approximate boundary within which the load is unlikely to create a risk of injury sufficient to warrant a detailed assessment.

6   Application of the guidelines will provide a reasonable level of protection to around 95% of working men and women. However, the guidelines should not be regarded as safe weight limits for lifting. There is no threshold below which manual handling operations may be regarded as 'safe'. Even operations lying within the boundary mapped out by the guidelines should be avoided or made less demanding wherever it is reasonably practicable to do so.

Using the filter

7   The filter is in several parts, covering lifting and lowering, frequent lifting, carrying, twisting, carrying, pushing and pulling and handling when seated. Use the guideline figures in each part to help you assess the task.

8   You will need to carry out a more detailed assessment (see Appendix 4) if:

(a)   using the filter shows the activity exceeds the guideline figures;

(b) the activities do not come within the guidelines, eg if lifting and lowering unavoidably takes place beyond the box zones in Figure 23;

(c) there are other considerations to take into account;

(d) the assumptions made in the filter are not applicable, for example when carrying the load it is not held against the body;

(e) for each task the assessment cannot be done quickly.

9   Paragraphs 28-29 and Table 3 provide an aide memoire for recording the findings from using the filter and reaching a judgement whether or not a full assessment is required.

Lifting and lowering

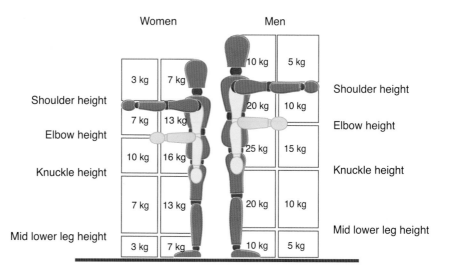

Figure 23 Lifting and lowering

10   Each box in the diagram contains a guideline weight for lifting and lowering in that zone. Using the diagram enables the assessor to take into account the vertical and horizontal position of the hands as they move the load, the height of the individual handler and the reach of the individual handler. As can be seen from the diagram, the guideline weights are reduced if handling is done with arms extended, or at high or low levels, as that is where injuries are most likely.

11   Observe the work activity being assessed and compare it to the diagram. First decide which box or boxes the lifter's hands pass through when moving the load. Then assess the maximum weight being handled. If it is less than the figure given in the box, the operation is within the guidelines.

12   If the lifter's hands enter more than one box during the operation, then the smallest weight figure applies. An intermediate weight can be chosen if the hands are close to a boundary between boxes.

13   The guideline figures for lifting and lowering assume:

(a) the load is easy to grasp with both hands;

(b) the operation takes place in reasonable working conditions; and

(c) the handler is in a stable body position.

14 If these assumptions are not valid, it will be necessary to make a full assessment as in Appendix 4.

Frequent lifting and lowering

15 The basic guideline figures for lifting and lowering in Figure 23 are for relatively infrequent operations – up to approximately 30 operations per hour or one lift every two minutes. The guideline figures will have to be reduced if the operation is repeated more often. As a rough guide:

Where operations are repeated	Figures should be reduced by
Once or twice per minute	30%
Five to eight times per minute	50%
More than 12 times per minute	80%

16 Even if the above conditions are satisfied, a more detailed risk assessment should be made where:

(a) the worker does not control the pace of work;

(b) pauses for rest are inadequate or there is no change of activity which provides an opportunity to use different muscles; or

(c) the handler must support the load for any length of time.

Twisting

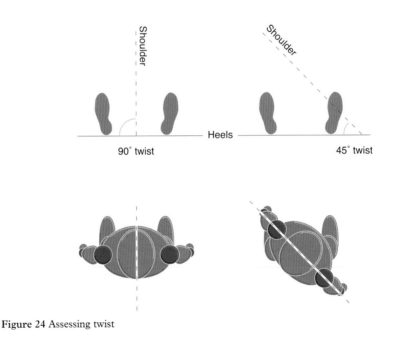

Figure 24 Assessing twist

17 In many cases manual handling operations will involve some twisting, ie moving the upper body while keeping the feet static (see Figure 24). The combination of twisting and lifting and twisting, stooping and lifting are particularly stressful on the back. Therefore where the handling involves twisting and turning then a detailed assessment should normally be made.

18   However if the operation is:

(a)   relatively infrequent (up to approximately 30 operations per hour or one lift every two minutes); and

(b)   there are no other posture problems,

then the guideline figures in the relevant part of this filter can be used, but with a suitable reduction according to the amount the handler twists to the side during the operation. As a rough guide:

If handler twists through (from front)	Guideline figures (Figure 24) should be reduced by
45°	10%
90°	20%

19   Where the handling involves turning, ie moving in another direction as the lift is in progress and twisting, then a detailed assessment should normally be made.

Guidelines for carrying

20   The guideline figures for lifting and lowering (Figure 23) apply to carrying operations where the load is:

(a)   held against the body;

(b)   carried no further than about 10 m without resting.

21   Where the load can be carried securely on the shoulder without first having to be lifted (as, for example when unloading sacks from a lorry) the guideline figures can be applied to carrying distances in excess of 10 m.

22   A more detailed assessment should be made for all carrying operations if:

(a)   the load is carried over a longer distance without resting; or

(b)   the hands are below knuckle height or above elbow height (due to static loading on arm muscles).

Guidelines for pushing and pulling

23   For pushing and pulling operations (whether the load is slid, rolled or supported on wheels) the guideline figures assume the force is applied with the hands, between knuckle and shoulder height. It is also assumed that the distance involved is no more than about 20 m. If these assumptions are not met, a more detailed risk assessment is required (see the push/pull checklist in Appendix 4).

	Men	Women
Guideline figure for stopping or starting a load	20 kg (ie about 200 newtons)	15 kg (ie about 150 newtons)
Guideline figure for keeping the load in motion	10 kg (ie about 100 newtons)	7 kg (ie about 70 newtons)

24   As a rough guide the amount of force that needs to be applied to move a load over a flat, level surface using a well-maintained handling aid is at least 2% of the load weight. For example, if the load weight is 400 kg, then the force needed to move the load is 8 kg. The force needed will be larger, perhaps a lot larger, if conditions are not perfect (eg wheels not in the right position or a device that is poorly maintained). Moving an object over soft or uneven surfaces also requires higher forces. On an uneven surface, the force needed to start the load moving could increase to 10% of the load weight, although this might be offset to some extent by using larger wheels. Pushing and pulling forces will also be increased if workers have to negotiate a slope or ramp (see paragraph 164 in the main document). **Even where the guideline figures in paragraph 23 are met, a detailed risk assessment will be necessary if risk factors such as uneven floors, confined spaces, or trapping hazards are present.**

25   There is no specific limit to the distance over which the load is pushed or pulled as long as there are adequate opportunities for rest or recovery. Refer to the push/pull checklist (see Appendix 4) if you are unsure and carry out a detailed risk assessment.

Guidelines for handling while seated

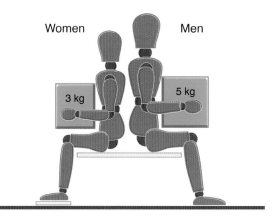

Figure 25 Handling while seated

26   The basic guideline figures for handling operations carried out while seated, shown in Figure 25, are:

Men	**Women**
5 kg	3 kg

27   These guidelines only apply when the hands are within the box zone indicated. If handling beyond the box zone is unavoidable, a more detailed assessment should be made.

Recording findings and reaching a decision

28   For each task, use the filter to assess each of the activities involved (some tasks may only involve one activity, eg lifting and lowering, while others may

involve several). Table 3 can be used to record the results; this is not a legal requirement but may be useful if problems later on are associated with the task.

29   Identify if each activity being performed comes within the guidelines and if there are other considerations to take into account (it may be helpful to make a note of these). Then make a final judgement of whether the task needs a full risk assessment. Remember you should be able to do this quickly - if not then a full risk assessment is required (see Appendix 4).

Table 3 Application of guidelines

Task:...			
Activity	For each activity, does the task fall outside the guidelines? Y/N	Are there any other considerations which indicate a problem? Y/N (Indicate what the problem is, if desired.)	Is a more detailed assessment required? Y/N
Lifting and lowering			
Carrying			
Pushing and pulling			
Handling while seated			

Limitations of the filter

30   **Remember:** The use of these guidelines does not affect the employer's duty to avoid or reduce the risk of injury where this is reasonably practicable. The guideline figures, therefore, should **not be regarded as weight limits or approved figures for safe lifting**. They are an aid to highlight where detailed risk assessments are most needed. Where doubt remains, a more detailed risk assessment should always be made.

31   The employer's primary duty is to avoid operations which involve a risk of injury or, where it is not practicable to do so, to assess each such operation and reduce the risk of injury to the lowest level reasonably practicable. As the probability of injury rises, the employer must scrutinise the operation increasingly closely with a view to a proper assessment and the reduction of the risk of injury to the lowest level reasonably practicable. Even for a minority of fit, well-trained individuals working under favourable conditions, operations which exceed the guideline figures by more than a factor of about two may represent a serious risk of injury.

Appendix 4   Examples of assessment checklists for lifting and carrying and pushing and pulling

1   A suitable and sufficient risk assessment is required when hazardous manual handling is unavoidable. The assessment should identify where the risk lies and identify an appropriate range of ideas for reducing the potential for injury. A checklist can help with this process by applying a systematic examination of all the potential risk elements. To ensure that the assessment covers all potential risks the workforce should be fully involved in the risk assessment process.

2   Examples of basic checklists for lifting and carrying and pushing and pulling are included in this appendix. Their use will help to highlight the overall level of risk involved and identify how the job may be modified to reduce the risk of injury and make it easier to do. It will also be useful in helping to prioritise the remedial actions needed. The checklists may be copied freely or may be used to help design your own assessment checklist.

3   The following notes are intended to help you complete the checklist.

(a)   **Section A: *Describe*** the job. There is space available for a diagram to be drawn to summarise the task in a picture, as well as for a written description.

(b)   **Section B: *Tick*** the level of risk you believe to be associated with each of the items on the list. Space is provided for noting the precise nature of the problem and for suggestions about the remedial action that may be taken. It may also be useful to write down the names of the relevant people or groups in your organisation who you will wish to consult about implementing the remedial steps, for example managers, workforce trainers, maintenance personnel or engineers and relevant employees or their safety representatives.

If you are assessing a lifting, carrying or team-handling operation and need help in judging the level of risk, you can consider using the MAC (Appendix 5) to help you decide the risk levels to be entered in Section B of the checklist.

Some tasks may involve more than one operator, each with a different level of risk, depending on the exact nature of their duties. If you wish to use the same checklist for all of the operators involved, you can allocate a number (or other identifying mark) to each and use that against each tick. Alternatively you can use a separate checklist for each operator.

(c)   ***Decide*** whether the overall risk of injury is low, medium or high. This will help to prioritise remedial action if you have a large number of risk assessments to carry out. Ring the appropriate word at the bottom of Section A after you have completed Section B.

(d)   **Section C: *Summarise*** the remedial steps that should be taken, in order of priority. The assessor's name, the name of the person responsible for carrying out any remedial action and the date by which such action should be completed should be recorded. Only once such action has been taken should the final column be completed. It may also be useful to enter the target date for reassessment if this is appropriate. Remember to check that any actions taken have the desired effect.

4   When all the manual handling tasks have been assessed, the completed checklists can be compared to help prioritise the most urgent actions. However, there are likely to be several ways to reduce the risks identified and some will be more effective than others. Action on those that can be implemented easily and quickly should not be delayed simply because they may be less effective than others.

5   A check should be carried out at a later date to ensure that the remedial action to remove or reduce the risk of injury has been effective.

6   Worked examples of risk assessments are included to show how the checklists might be used in practice.

7   The purpose of the checklists is to help bring out a range of ideas on how the risks identified can be avoided or reduced by making modifications to the load, the task, and the working environment. Many suggestions for reducing risks in particular situations are given in the text of this booklet. There are also a number of people who may be able to help with suggestions, for example safety representatives, the quality management team within the organisation, and relevant trade associations. There is also a great deal of other published information about risk-reduction methods. *Manual handling: Solutions you can handle*[23] and *A pain in your workplace*,[24] both published by HSE, give examples that are relevant to situations across many sectors of industry. Trade journals also often contain information about products that can be used to help reduce the risk of injury from the manual handling of loads.

Manual handling of loads: Assessment checklist

Section A - Preliminary

Task name: Task description: Load weight: Frequency of lift: Carry distances (if applicable): Are other manual handling tasks carried out by these operators? Assessment discussed with employees/safety representatives:	Is an assessment needed? (An assessment will be needed if there is a potential risk of injury, eg if the task falls outside the guidelines in Appendix 3.) Yes/No* *Circle as appropriate

If 'Yes' continue. If 'No' the assessment need go no further.

Operations covered by this assessment (detailed description): Locations: Personnel involved: Date of assessment:	Diagrams (other information including existing control measures):

Overall assessment of the risk of injury? *Circle as appropriate	Low/ Medium/ High*

Make your overall assessment **after** you have completed Section B.

Section B: Lifting and carrying - More detailed assessment, where necessary

Questions to consider:	If yes, tick appropriate level of risk			Problems occurring from the task (Make rough notes in this column in preparation for the possible remedial action to be taken)	Possible remedial action, eg changes that need to be made to the task, load, working environment etc. Who needs to be involved in implementing the changes?
	Low	Med	High		
Do **the tasks** involve:					
● holding loads away from trunk?					
● twisting?					
● stooping?					
● reaching upwards?					
● large vertical movement?					
● long carrying distances?					
● strenuous pushing or pulling?					
● unpredictable movement of loads?					
● repetitive handling?					
● insufficient rest or recovery?					
● a work rate imposed by a process?					
Are **the loads:**					
●heavy?					
●bulky/unwieldy?					
●difficult to grasp?					
●unstable/unpredictable?					
●intrinsically harmful (eg sharp/hot)?					

Section B: Lifting and carrying - More detailed assessment, where necessary

Questions to consider:	If yes, tick appropriate level of risk			Problems occurring from the task (Make rough notes in this column in preparation for the possible remedial action to be taken)	Possible remedial action, eg changes that need to be made to the task, load, working environment etc. Who needs to be involved in implementing the changes?
	Low	Med	High		
Consider **the working environment** - are there:					
• constraints on posture?					
• poor floors?					
• variations in levels?					
• hot/cold/humid conditions?					
• strong air movements?					
• poor lighting conditions?					
Consider **individual capability** - does the job:					
• require unusual capability?					
• pose a risk to those with a health problem or a physical or learning difficulty?					
• pose a risk to those who are pregnant?					
• call for special information/training?					

Section B: Lifting and carrying – More detailed assessment, where necessary

Questions to consider:	Yes/No	Problems occurring from the task (Make rough notes in this column in preparation for the possible remedial action to be taken)	Possible remedial action, eg changes that need to be made to the task, load, working environment etc. Who needs to be involved in implementing the changes?
Other factors to consider			
Protective clothing			
● Is movement or posture hindered by clothing or personal protective equipment?	Yes/No		
● Is there an absence of the correct/suitable PPE being worn?	Yes/No		
Work organisation (psychosocial factors)			
● Do workers feel that there has been a lack of consideration given to the planning and scheduling of tasks/rest breaks?	Yes/No		
● Do workers feel that there is poor communication between managers and employees (eg not involved in risk assessments or decisions on changes in workstation design)?	Yes/No		
● Are there sudden changes in workload, or seasonal changes in volume without mechanisms for dealing with the change?	Yes/No		
● Do workers feel they have not been given enough training and information to carry out the task successfully?	Yes/No		

Section C - Remedial action to be taken

Remedial steps that should be taken, in order of priority:	Person responsible for implementing controls	Target implementation date	Completed Y/N
1			
2			
3			
4			
5			
6			
7			
8			
9			
Date by which actions should be completed:			
Date for review of assessment:			
Assessor's name: Signature:			

TAKE ACTION . . . AND CHECK THAT IT HAS THE DESIRED EFFECT

Manual handling of loads: Assessment checklist worked example

Section A - Preliminary

Task name: *Conveyor/pallet loading* Task description: *Pallet loading: boxes containing coiled wire. Remove from conveyor onto pallet.* Load weight: *45 kg* Frequency of lift: *15 lifts/hour* Carry distances (if applicable): *3 m* Are other manual handling tasks carried out by these operators? *No* Assessment discussed with employees/safety representatives: *Yes*	Is an assessment needed? (An assessment will be needed if there is a potential risk of injury, eg if the task falls outside the guidelines in Appendix 3.) (Yes)/No★ ★Circle as appropriate

If 'Yes' continue. If 'No' the assessment need go no further.

Operations covered by this assessment (detailed description): *Operator lifts box, with hook grip, from conveyor, which is 50 cm above the ground, turns, walks 3 m and lowers box onto a pallet on the ground. Boxes are piled six high on pallet.* Locations: *Wire factory only* Personnel involved: *One operator* Date of assessment: *24 June 2004*	Diagrams (other information including existing control measures): *(a) Worker* *(b) Conveyor* *(c) 45 kg boxes of wire* *(d) Pallet* *Arrows show direction of conveyor belt and worker movements between conveyor and pallet*

Overall assessment of the risk of injury? ★Circle as appropriate	Low/ Medium/(High★)

Make your overall assessment **after** you have completed Section B.

Section B: Lifting and carrying – More detailed assessment, where necessary

Questions to consider:	If yes, tick appropriate level of risk			Problems occurring from the task (Make rough notes in this column in preparation for the possible remedial action to be taken)	Possible remedial action, eg changes that need to be made to the task, load, working environment etc. Who needs to be involved in implementing the changes?
	Low	Med	High		
Do the tasks involve:					
● holding loads away from trunk?			✓	1 Twisting when picking up the box.	Remind operator of need to move feet.
● twisting?		✓			
● stooping?			✓	2 Stooping when placing box on pallet and stooping when picking box up from the conveyor.	Adjust pallet height – Review availability of rotating, height adjusting equipment and raise height of conveyor.
● reaching upwards?	✓				
● large vertical movement?	✓				
● long carrying distances?	✓			3 Sometimes extended reaching when placing boxes on pallet.	Provide better information and instruction.
● strenuous pushing or pulling?	✓				
● unpredictable movement of loads?	✓				
● repetitive handling?	✓				Review mechanical handling equipment to eliminate manual lifting.
● insufficient rest or recovery?	✓				
● a work rate imposed by a process?	✓				
Are the loads:					
● heavy?			✓	4 Load too heavy. Is the weight of the load a problem for customers too?	Review product and customer needs with a view to improving product design.
● bulky/unwieldy?	✓				
● difficult to grasp?		✓		5 Smooth cardboard boxes are difficult to grasp.	Provide boxes with hand grips.
● unstable/unpredictable?	✓				
● intrinsically harmful (eg sharp/hot)?	✓				

Section B: Lifting and carrying - More detailed assessment, where necessary

Questions to consider:	If yes, tick appropriate level of risk			Problems occurring from the task (Make rough notes in this column in preparation for the possible remedial action to be taken)	Possible remedial action, eg changes that need to be made to the task, load, working environment etc. Who needs to be involved in implementing the changes?
	Low	Med	High		
Consider **the working environment** - are there:					
● constraints on posture?		✓		6 *Bad postures encouraged by*	*Introduce system to ensure full pallets*
● poor floors?	✓			*obstructions when full pallets are not*	*removed promptly – Speak to Operations*
● variations in levels?	✓			*removed.*	*Manager.*
● hot/cold/humid conditions?	✓				
● strong air movements?	✓				
● poor lighting conditions?	✓				
Consider **individual capability** - does the job:					
● require unusual capability?			✓	7 *Operator has no history of back pain*	*Consider job enlargement to introduce*
● pose a risk to those with a health problem or a physical or learning difficulty?			✓	*problems but clear signs of sweating and straining.*	*variety and allow for recovery time.* *Monitor to ensure no rushing.*
● pose a risk to those who are pregnant?			✓		*Speak to trainer about manual handling*
● call for special information/training?		✓			*course.*

Section B: Lifting and carrying – More detailed assessment, where necessary

Questions to consider:	Yes/No	Problems occurring from the task (Make rough notes in this column in preparation for the possible remedial action to be taken)	Possible remedial action, eg changes that need to be made to the task, load, working environment etc. Who needs to be involved in implementing the changes?
Other factors to consider			
Protective clothing			
● Is movement or posture hindered by clothing or personal protective equipment?	Yes/No		
● Is there an absence of the correct/suitable PPE being worn?	Yes/No		
Work organisation (psychosocial factors)			
● Do workers feel that there has been a lack of consideration given to the planning and scheduling of tasks/rest breaks?	Yes/No	8 Boxes delivered at pre-set rate.	Look at varying delivery rate.
● Do workers feel that there is poor communication between managers and employees (eg not involved in risk assessments or decisions on changes in workstation design)?	Yes/No	9 Employees not directly involved in risk assessment process.	Discussions to be held with safety representatives and other workers during identification and when solutions are decided.
● Are there sudden changes in workload, or seasonal changes in volume without mechanisms for dealing with the change?	Yes/No		
● Do workers feel they have not been given enough training and information to carry out the task successfully?	Yes/No		

70

Section C - Remedial action to be taken

Remedial steps that should be taken, in order of priority:	Person responsible for implementing controls	Target implementation date	Completed Y/N
1 Safety representatives and employees to be involved in risk assessment process and workstation design.	A N Onymous	ASAP	Yes
2 Review product design to reduce weight of load and improve grip.	A N Onymous	Jul 2004	Yes
3 Review process in light of changes agreed in (1), particularly on customer requirements and transportation.	A N Onymous	Aug 2004	Yes
4 Seek funding for magnetic lifting aid to help with transfer from conveyor to pallet.	A N Onymous	Aug 2004	Yes
5 Seek funding for pallet rotating/height adjustment equipment.	A N Onymous	Aug 2004	Yes
6 Operator to attend manual handling training.	A N Onymous	Sept 2004	Yes
7 Raise conveyor height by 35 cm.	A N Onymous	Sept 2004	Yes
8 Ensure full pallets are removed by pallet truck promptly.	A N Onymous	Ongoing	Yes
9 Operations manager to ensure no rushing on this job.	A N Onymous	Ongoing	Yes

Date by which actions should be completed: 30 Nov 2004

Date for review of assessment: 15 April 2005

Assessor's name: A N Onymous   Signature: A N Onymous

TAKE ACTION . . . AND CHECK THAT IT HAS THE DESIRED EFFECT

Pushing and pulling of loads: Assessment checklist

Section A - Preliminary

<table>
<tr>
<td>

Task name:

Task description:

Load weight:

Frequency of operation:

Push/pull distances:

Are other push/pull tasks carried out by these operators?

Assessment discussed with employees/safety representatives:

</td>
<td>

Is an assessment needed?
(An assessment will be needed if there is a potential risk of injury, eg if the task falls outside the guidelines in Appendix 3.)

Yes/No★

★Circle as appropriate

</td>
</tr>
</table>

If 'Yes' continue. If 'No' the assessment need go no further.

<table>
<tr>
<td>

Operations covered by this assessment (detailed description):

Locations:

Personnel involved:

Date of assessment:

</td>
<td>

Diagrams (other information including existing control measures):

</td>
</tr>
</table>

Overall assessment of the risk of injury?   Low/ Medium/ High★
★Circle as appropriate

Make your overall assessment **after** you have completed Section B.

Questions to consider:	If yes, tick appropriate level of risk			Problems occurring from the task (Make rough notes in this column in preparation for the possible remedial action to be taken)	Possible remedial action, eg changes that need to be made to the task, load, working environment etc. Who needs to be involved in implementing the changes?
	Low	Med	High		
Do **the tasks** involve:					
● high initial forces to get the load moving?					
● high forces to keep the load in motion?					
● sudden movements to start, stop or manoeuvre the load?					
● twisting/manoeuvring of the load into position or around obstacles?					
● one-handed operations?					
● the hands below the waist or above shoulder height?					
● movement at high speed?					
● movement over long distances?					
● repetitive pushing/pulling?					
The **load or object** to be moved:					
● does it lack good handholds?					
● is it unstable/unpredictable?					
● is vision over/around it restricted?					
If on wheels/castors, are they:					
● unsuitable for the type of load?					
● unsuitable for the floor surface/work environment?					
● difficult to steer?					
● easily damaged or defective?					
● without brakes or difficult to stop?					
● with brakes, but the brakes are poor/ineffective?					
● without a planned inspection and maintenance regime based on a frequency that keeps them in working order?					

Section B: Pushing and pulling - More detailed assessment, where necessary

Questions to consider:	If yes, tick appropriate level of risk			Problems occurring from the task (Make rough notes in this column in preparation for the possible remedial action to be taken)	Possible remedial action, eg changes that need to be made to the task, load, working environment etc. Who needs to be involved in implementing the changes?
	Low	Med	High		
Consider **the working environment** - are there:					
• constraints on body posture/positioning?					
• confined spaces/narrow doorways?					
• surfaces or edges to cause cuts/abrasions/burns to hands or body?					
• rutted/damaged/slippery floors?					
• ramps/slopes/uneven surfaces?					
• trapping or tripping hazards?					
• poor lighting conditions?					
• hot/cold/humid conditions?					
• strong air movements?					
Consider **individual capability** - does the job:					
• require unusual capability?					
• hazard those with a health problem or a physical or learning difficulty?					
• hazard those who are pregnant?					
• call for special information/training?					

Questions to consider:	Yes/No	Problems occurring from the task (Make rough notes in this column in preparation for the possible remedial action to be taken)	Possible remedial action, eg changes that need to be made to the task, load, working environment etc. Who needs to be involved in implementing the changes?
Other factors to consider			
Equipment			
• Is movement or posture hindered by clothing or personal protective equipment?	Yes/No		
• Is there an absence of the correct/suitable PPE being worn?	Yes/No		
• Are trolleys/carts/floor surfaces poorly maintained/cleaned/repaired?	Yes/No		
• Is there a lack of a regular maintenance procedures for the equipment?	Yes/No		
Work organisation			
• Do workers feel that there has been a lack of consideration given to the planning and scheduling of tasks/rest breaks?	Yes/No		
• Do workers feel that there is poor communication between users of equipment and others (eg managers, purchasers etc)?	Yes/No		
• Are there sudden changes in workload, or seasonal changes in volume without mechanisms for dealing with the change?	Yes/No		
• Do workers feel they have not been given enough training and information to carry out the task successfully?	Yes/No		

Section C - Remedial action to be taken

Remedial steps that should be taken, in order of priority:	Person responsible for implementing controls	Target implementation date	Completed Y/N
1			
2			
3			
4			
5			
6			
7			
8			
9			
Date by which actions should be completed:			
Date for review of assessment:			
Assessor's name: Signature:			

TAKE ACTION . . . AND CHECK THAT IT HAS THE DESIRED EFFECT

Pushing and pulling of loads: Assessment checklist worked example

Section A - Preliminary

<table>
<tr>
<td>

Task name: *Collecting bins*

Task description: *Collecting waste paper from computer company using industrial refuse bins*

Load weight: *Can exceed 25 kg*

Frequency of operation: *1 push/pull every 5-10 mins*

Push/pull distances: *Between 2-15 m depending on the location of the vehicle*

Are other push/pull tasks carried out by these operators? *No*

Assessment discussed with employees/safety representatives: *Yes*

</td>
<td>

Is an assessment needed?
(An assessment will be needed if there is a potential risk of injury, eg if the task falls outside the guidelines in Appendix 3.)

(Yes)/No★

★Circle as appropriate

</td>
</tr>
</table>

If 'Yes' continue. If 'No' the assessment need go no further.

<table>
<tr>
<td>

Operations covered by this assessment (detailed description): *Operator leaves vehicle and walks to bin storage area. Operator must then pull fully laden bin from storage area and push/pull load around vehicles parked in car park outside storage area. Once contents have been removed, bin is pushed/pulled back into storage area.*

Locations: *Storage bin area*

Personnel involved: *One operator*

Date of assessment: *23 Jan 2004*

</td>
<td>

Diagrams (other information including existing control measures):

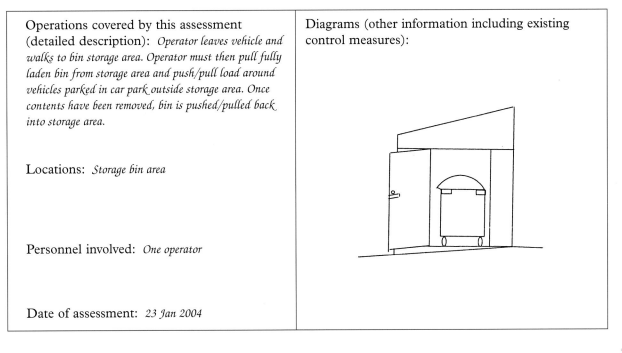

</td>
</tr>
</table>

Overall assessment of the risk of injury?   Low/(Medium)/High★
★Circle as appropriate

Make your overall assessment **after** you have completed Section B.

Section B: Pushing and pulling – More detailed assessment, where necessary

Questions to consider:	Low	Med	High	Problems occurring from the task (Make rough notes in this column in preparation for the possible remedial action to be taken)	Possible remedial action, eg changes that need to be made to the task, load, working environment etc. Who needs to be involved in implementing the changes?
Do **the tasks** involve:					
• high initial forces to get the load moving?			✓	1 Initially the wheels are often difficult to move as they may be inappropriately aligned, the refuse bin may have been unattended for some time, and debris builds up around wheels.	*Remind operators to check position and alignment of wheels, and whether there is debris or obstructions which may inhibit their movement. Assess suitability of bin/wheels for the type of location. Inform customers.*
• high forces to keep the load in motion?		✓			
• sudden movements to start, stop or manoeuvre the load?			✓		
• twisting/manoeuvring of the load into position or around obstacles?			✓		
• one-handed operations?	✓			2 Close parking of cars near refuse bins and restricted space in storage areas leads to pushing/pulling with twisted postures.	*Remind operators of importance of clearing suitable path for bin. Review instructions and training on manual handling techniques.*
• the hands below the waist or above shoulder height?	✓				
• movement at high speed?	✓				
• movement over long distances?			✓	3 Difficulties of parking the collection vehicle close to refuse bins.	*Review scheduling of collection rounds and information supplied to customers on the positioning of bins.*
• repetitive pushing/pulling?			✓		
The **load or object** to be moved:					
• does it lack good handholds?		✓		4 Bins are often overfilled. Compact/dense material (eg computer paper) leads to heavy loads.	*Discuss with customers the reasons for bins being overfilled and examine feasibility of providing additional bins.*
• is it unstable/unpredictable?		✓			
• is vision over/around it restricted?		✓			
If on wheels/castors, are they:					
• unsuitable for the type of load?	✓			5 Overfilled bins can restrict visibility.	*Instruct operators to remove excess contents (but warn not to lift awkward or heavy objects) and/or seek assistance when moving bins.*
• unsuitable for the floor surface/work environment?	✓				
• difficult to steer?			✓	6 The four swivel castors make the bin difficult to handle on sloping ground and when moving over long distances.	*Review the suitability and practicality of fitting castors with a swivel locking mechanism. Assess design of bins/handles/wheel brakes. Ensure handle heights are appropriate.*
• easily damaged or defective?		✓			
• without brakes or difficult to stop?					
• with brakes, but the brakes are poor/ineffective?		✓			
• without a planned inspection and maintenance regime based on a frequency that keeps them in working order?		✓			

Section B: Pushing and pulling – More detailed assessment, where necessary

Questions to consider:	If yes, tick appropriate level of risk			Problems occurring from the task (Make rough notes in this column in preparation for the possible remedial action to be taken)	Possible remedial action, eg changes that need to be made to the task, load, working environment etc. Who needs to be involved in implementing the changes?
	Low	Med	High		
Consider **the working environment** – are there:					
● constraints on body posture/positioning?		✓		7 Storage areas, waste material and obstructions often inhibit the ease with which the bin can be moved.	Review storage area facilities to ensure clear access to bins during pickups.
● confined spaces/narrow doorways?		✓			
● surfaces or edges to cause cuts/abrasions/burns to hands or body?			✓		
● rutted/damaged/slippery floors?		✓		8 A marked step between doorway frame and the ground outside the store room. Terrain uneven and noticeable camber.	Make customers aware of difficulties and seek to improve access, particularly outside the store room.
● ramps/slopes/uneven surfaces?			✓		
● trapping or tripping hazards?		✓			
● poor lighting conditions?		✓			
● hot/cold/humid conditions?		✓		9 Variable weather conditions and hazardous terrain. Special problems during snow/ice.	Ensure operators have appropriate footwear and protective equipment/clothing, particularly for adverse weather conditions.
● strong air movements?		✓			
Consider **individual capability** – does the job:					
● require unusual capability?		✓		10 Those suffering from musculoskeletal and respiratory complaints are likely to encounter difficulties when they carry out the work.	Review training to ensure that operators are aware of the risks. Ensure employees are given suitable induction training and appropriate systems for reporting complaints are in place. Review procedures for return to work following health problems.
● hazard those with a health problem or a physical or learning difficulty?			✓		
● hazard those who are pregnant?			✓		
● call for special information/training?		✓			

Section B: Pushing and pulling – More detailed assessment, where necessary

Questions to consider:	Yes/No	Problems occurring from the task (Make rough notes in this column in preparation for the possible remedial action to be taken)	Possible remedial action, eg changes that need to be made to the task, load, working environment etc. Who needs to be involved in implementing the changes?
Other factors to consider *Equipment*			
• Is movement or posture hindered by clothing or personal protective equipment?	Yes/No		
• Is there an absence of the correct/suitable PPE being worn?	Yes/No		
• Are trolleys/carts/floor surfaces poorly maintained/cleaned/repaired?	Yes/No	11 *Refuse collectors have a tendency not to report problems.*	*Review reporting procedures to actively encourage the reporting of breakage/failure of refuse bins.*
• Is there a lack of a regular maintenance procedures for the equipment?	Yes/No	12 *When a problem is reported, it is not always apparent that action is taken.*	*Implement a formal method to document problems and review maintenance procedures.*
Work organisation			
• Do workers feel that there has been a lack of consideration given to the planning and scheduling of tasks/rest breaks?	Yes/No		
• Do workers feel that there is poor communication between users of equipment and others (eg managers, purchasers etc)?	Yes/No	13 *Refuse collectors feel that they are not consulted about good features of bin design that aid handling tasks.*	*Review procedures for facilitating discussions between user and equipment purchasers.*
• Are there sudden changes in workload, or seasonal changes in volume without mechanisms for dealing with the change?	Yes/No		
• Do workers feel they have not been given enough training and information to carry out the task successfully?	Yes/No		

Section C - Remedial action to be taken

Remedial steps that should be taken, in order of priority:	Person responsible for implementing controls	Target implementation date	Completed Y/N
1 Discuss and agree with customers improvements to ground directly outside storage area.	A N Onymous	20 Feb 2004	Yes
2 Discuss and agree with customers appropriate steps to prevent overfilling of bins - review its effectiveness.	A N Onymous	25 Feb 2004	Yes
3 Review storage facilities to improve ease of access to bins and discuss with customers arrangements for good housekeeping practices.	A N Onymous	28 Feb 2004	Yes
4 Operator to attend relevant manual handling training course.	A N Onymous	25 March 2004	Yes
5 Instigate a reporting procedure to encourage workers to report problems. Ensure that a system of work is in place to address and monitor these problems.	A N Onymous	30 March 2004	Yes
6 Review refuse bin design to ensure that it is most suited to customer needs and handling requirements, eg size and shape in view of waste contents, wheel/castor design characteristics. Seek funding to replace/modify bin design, if required.	A N Onymous	25 April 2004	Yes
7 Ensure the provision of suitable clothing and footwear.	A N Onymous	30 April 2004	Yes
8			
9			

Date by which actions should be completed: *31 May 2004*

Date for review of assessment: *15 December 2004*

Assessor's name: *A N Onymous*   Signature: *A N Onymous*

TAKE ACTION . . . AND CHECK THAT IT HAS THE DESIRED EFFECT

Appendix 5   Manual handling assessment chart (MAC)

1   The MAC, which is described below, is a new assessment tool that has been developed by HSE. It is principally designed to help health and safety inspectors assess the most common risk factors in lifting, carrying and team handling operations. Employers, safety officers, safety representatives and others may also find the MAC useful to identify high-risk manual handling operations and help them as part of their risk assessments.

2   Copies of the MAC are available as a free leaflet (INDG383) for single copies and priced for multiple copies, from HSE books. The MAC can also be printed from the following website: www.hse.gov.uk/msd/mac. However the MAC is **not** appropriate for all manual handling operations, and so may **not** comprise a fully 'suitable and sufficient' risk assessment if relied on alone. A risk assessment will normally need to take account of additional factors, for example an individual's health problems or the need for special information and training. The rest of this document sets out in detail the requirements of an assessment.

3   The MAC is based on a set of numerical guidelines developed from data in published scientific literature and on practical experience of assessing risks from manual handling. They are pragmatic, tried and tested and are not based on any precise scientific formulae. The intention is to guide users through a logical process to identify any high-risk manual handling.

4   The MAC comprises a series of manual handling assessment charts designed for quickly assessing the following:

(a)   lifting operations;

(b)   carrying operations; and

(c)   team-handling operations.

5   The MAC is not suitable for tasks which involve pushing and pulling and for assessing the risk involved in patient handling.

6   The MAC uses a 'traffic light' approach for indicating the level of risk. A numerical indication is also provided. The risk levels are based on published ergonomic data and are the same as those used within the rest of this guidance.

7   Each chart in the MAC requires the user to work through a sequence of risk factors, beginning with load and lifting/carrying frequency. For the lifting chart, the following factors are then considered in turn:

(a)   the position of the hands horizontally in relation to the lower back;

(b)   the vertical lift distance;

(c)   the degree of twisting:

(d)   postural constraints;

(e)   the quality of the grip;

(f)   floor conditions; and

(g)   other environmental factors.

8   Similar considerations apply in the carrying and team handling charts.

9   Individual characteristics such as age, sex, physical fitness, strength and psychosocial factors are **not** included on the chart, but should be considered when completing the score sheet.

10   Total numerical scores should be used to assist the assessor with their prioritisation of remedial actions. The scores provide an indication of which manual handling tasks require attention first. The scores should only be used for comparison purposes since the total scores do not relate to objective action levels. The scores can also be used as a way of evaluating potential improvements. Generally the most effective improvements will bring about the highest reduction in the score.

11   The primary aim of the MAC is to act as an aid to identifying high-risk activities for which urgent further action is necessary:

(a)   Purple or red scores for any risk factor are generally considered to imply a high risk of injury needing prompt action to reduce the risk. It is likely to be worth taking such action immediately, then resuming the risk assessment process from the beginning to check that the action taken has been successful and that no other significant risks remain.

(b)   Amber scores generally require a more detailed assessment, looking at the scope for reducing the overall risk.

(c)   Task components with green scores are generally considered to have a low level of risk. The vulnerability of special risk groups (eg pregnant and young workers) should be considered where appropriate. However, it should be remembered that there is no threshold below which manual handling operations may be regarded as 'safe'. Even operations lying within the green zone should be avoided or made less demanding wherever it is reasonably practicable to do so.

References

1   *Health and Safety (Miscellaneous Amendments) Regulations 2002*
SI 2002/2174 The Stationery Office 2002 ISBN 0 11 042693 2

2   *Health and Safety at Work etc Act 1974 Ch37* The Stationery Office 1974
ISBN 0 10 543774 3

3   The EC Directive on manual handling: Council Directive of 29 May
1990 on the minimum health and safety requirements for the manual handling
of loads where there is a risk particularly of back injury to workers (fourth
individual Directive within the meaning of Article 16(1) of Directive
89/391/EEC) (90/269/EEC)) *Official Journal of the European Communities*,
21 June 1990, Vol 33, No L156 9-13

4   *Management of health and safety at work. Management of Health and Safety
at Work Regulations 1999. Approved Code of Practice and guidance* L21 (Second
edition) HSE Books 2000 ISBN 0 7176 2488 9

5   *Upper limb disorders in the workplace* HSG60 (Second edition) HSE Books
2002 ISBN 0 7176 1978 8

6   *The back book* (Second edition) The Stationery Office 2002
ISBN 0 11 702949 1

7   *Safety representatives and safety committees* L87 (Third edition) HSE Books
1996 ISBN 0 7176 1220 1

8   *A guide to the Health and Safety (Consultation with Employees) Regulations
1996. Guidance on Regulations* L95 HSE Books 1996 ISBN 0 7176 1234 1

9   *Control of substances hazardous to health. The Control of Substances
Hazardous to Health Regulations 2002. Approved Code of Practice and guidance*
L5 (Fourth edition) HSE Books 2002 ISBN 0 7176 2534 6

10   *Workplace health, safety and welfare. Workplace (Health, Safety and
Welfare) Regulations 1992. Approved Code of Practice* L24 HSE Books 1992
ISBN 0 7176 0413 6

11   *Handling home care: Achieving safe, efficient and positive outcomes for care
workers and clients* HSG225 HSE Books 2002 ISBN 0 7176 2228 2

12   *Safe use of work equipment. Provision and Use of Work Equipment
Regulations 1998. Approved Code of Practice and guidance* L22 (Second edition)
HSE Books 1998 ISBN 0 7176 1626 6

13   *Safe use of lifting equipment. Lifting Operations and Lifting Equipment
Regulations 1998. Approved Code of Practice and guidance* L113 HSE Books
1998 ISBN 0 7176 1628 2

14   *Roll cages and wheeled racks in the food and drink industries: Reducing
manual handling injuries* Food Information Sheet FIS33 HSE Books 2003

15   *Seating at work* HSG57 (Second edition) HSE Books 1997
ISBN 0 7176 1231 7

16   *Supply of Machinery (Safety) Regulations 1992* SI 1992/3073
The Stationery Office 1992 ISBN 0 11 025719 7 as amended by the *Supply of
Machinery (Safety) Amendment Regulations 1994* SI 1994/2063 The Stationery
Office 1994 ISBN 0 11 045063 9

17   *Disability Discrimination Act 1995* (c 50) The Stationery Office 1996 ISBN 0 10 545095 2

18   *New and expectant mothers at work: A guide for employers* HSG122 (Second edition) HSE Books 2002 ISBN 0 7176 2583 4

19   *Personal protective equipment at work. Personal Protective Equipment at Work Regulations 1992. Guidance on Regulations* L25 HSE Books 1992 ISBN 0 7176 0415 2

20   *The principles of good manual handling: Achieving a consensus* RR097 HSE Books 2003 ISBN 0 7176 2179 0

21   *Disability Discrimination Act 1995: Code of practice for the elimination of discrimination in the field of employment against disabled persons or persons who have had a disability* The Stationery Office 1996 ISBN 0 11 270954 0

22   *Health surveillance at work* HSG61 (Second edition) HSE Books 1999 ISBN 0 7176 1705 X

23   *Manual handling: Solutions you can handle* HSG115 HSE Books 1994 ISBN 0 7176 0693 7

24   *A pain in your workplace? Ergonomic problems and solutions* HSG121 HSE Books 1994 ISBN 0 7176 0668 6

Further reading

HSE publications

Getting to grips with handling problems: Worked examples of assessment and reduction of risk in the health services HSE Books 1994 ISBN 0 7176 0622 8

Getting to grips with manual handling: A short guide for employers Leaflet INDG143(rev1) HSE Books 2000 (single copy free or priced packs of 15 ISBN 0 7176 1754 8)

Guide to managing health and safety in paper mills Part 3: Manual handling in paper mills HSE Books 1998 ISBN 0 7176 0801 8

Handling and stacking bales in agriculture Leaflet INDG125(rev1) HSE Books 1998 (single copy free)

Handling rubber: Reducing manual handling injuries in the rubber industry Video HSE Books 1999 ISBN 0 7176 1854 4

Injuries and ill health caused by handling in the food and drink industries Food Information Sheet FIS23 HSE Books 2000

Lighting at work HSG38 (Second edition) HSE Books 1997 ISBN 0 7176 1232 5

Manual handling in drinks delivery HSG119 HSE Books 1994 ISBN 0 7176 0731 3

Manual handling in the health services (Second edition) HSE Books 1998 ISBN 0 7176 1248 1

Manual handling solutions for farms Leaflet AS23(rev2) HSE Books 2000 (single copy free)

Moving food and drink: Manual handling solutions for the food and drinks industries HSG196 HSE Books 2000 ISBN 0 7176 1731 9

Picking up the pieces: Prevention of musculoskeletal disorders in the ceramics industry HSE Books 1996 ISBN 0 7176 0872 7

Reducing injuries caused by sack handling in the food and drink industries Food Information Sheet FIS31 HSE Books 2001

Reducing manual handling injuries in the rubber industry: A practical guide HSE Books 1999 ISBN 0 7176 2466 8

Well handled: Offshore manual handling solutions HSG171 HSE Books 1997 ISBN 0 7176 1385 2

Other publications

Mital A and Nicholson AS *A guide to manual materials handling* (Second edition) Taylor and Francis 1997 ISBN 0 7484 0728 6

Pheasant S *Bodyspace: Anthropometry, ergonomics and the design of work* Taylor and Francis 1996 ISBN 0 7484 0067 2

Pheasant S *Ergonomics, work and health* Macmillan 1991 ISBN 0 333 48998 5

Pheasant S and Stubbs D *Lifting and handling: An ergonomic approach* National Back Pain Association 1991 ISBN 0 9507726 4 X

International Labour Office/International Ergonomics Association *Ergonomic checkpoints: Practical and easy-to-implement solutions for improving safety, health and working conditions* ILO publications 1996 ISBN 92 2 109442 1

National Back Pain Association/Royal College of Nursing *A guide to the handling of patients. Introducing a safer handling policy* (Fourth edition) 1997 ISBN 0 9530582 0 4

Useful contacts

The Ergonomics Society, Devonshire House, Devonshire Square, Loughborough, Leicestershire LE11 3DW
Tel: 01509 234904
Fax: 01509 235666
Website: www.ergonomics.org.uk

National Back Exchange, Linden Barns, Greens Norton Road, Towcester Northamptonshire NN12 8AW
Tel: 01327 358855
Fax: 01327 353778
Website: www.nationalbackexchange.org.uk

Institution of Occupational Safety and Health (IOSH), The Grange, Highfield Drive, Wigston, Leicestershire LE18 1NN
Tel: 0116 257 3100
Fax: 0116 257 3101
Website: www.iosh.co.uk

Further information

See inside back cover for details of how to obtain publications from HSE Books.

The Stationery Office (formerly HMSO) publications are available from The Publications Centre, PO Box 276, London SW8 5DT Tel: 0870 600 5522 Fax: 0870 600 5533 Website: www.tso.co.uk (They are also available from bookshops.)

Printed and published by the Health and Safety Executive   03/04   C200